Forty Days

9 Concepts for the Christian
from the Book of Jonah

I0571643

Emissary

ISBN 979-8-9905562-7-0

Published in Phoenix, Arizona by Emissary Publishing. Emissary is a business trade name of Ed's Voices, LLC.

Scripture quotations are taken from the King James Bible, unless otherwise cited/specified.

The views expressed by the author are those of the author and do not necessarily reflect the views of the publisher.

Praise For "Forty Days"

"Every child of God should be a student of the Word of God. Cory Sexton's book is a wonderful aid to help God's children better understand and use His Word. Cory's study on Jonah helped me, challenged me, and caused me to look up to God. I am grateful Cory is making this book available to all those desirous of knowing and growing in the Word."
Jeffrey Bush, Vision Baptist Missions President

"Cory Sexton offers clear and insightful Christian principles found in the story of Jonah that should shape the worldview of every believer. This is a must-read for anyone seeking a careful and comprehensive exploration of the book of Jonah.

"As a young teenager, I could tell you that the book of Jonah was found on page 1008 in my Scofield Bible. Like Christians through the ages, I have loved and read this story countless times. Cory Sexton has expanded my current understanding and provided insights I had never seen before in his latest book. This often-misunderstood historical event is frequently underutilized in Christian growth. Cory Sexton exposes nine principles that are non-negotiable in properly understanding the Christian life. I would highly recommend this book to anyone wanting to further their understanding of the story of Jonah. Additionally, I will recommend this book to new Bible students as it provides a wonderful example of how to rightly divide the truth from an Old Testament narrative."
Trent Cornwell
Pastor Vision Baptist Church

"My immediate impression from reading 'Forty Days – A Study of Jonah' is that it's a book well-suited for those seeking practical principles for the Christian life. One of the unique qualities found in this study of the book of Jonah is the hospitable nature it exudes through the pastoral warmth conveyed by the author. Bearing the warmth of devotion, it transcends mere devotional norms, embracing both theological and doxological heights. Both seasoned scholars and new believers will find value in this welcoming examination of the principles offered through a fresh look at the life of Jonah."

Zach Watson

Director of Refresh-Restore Ministries

Foreword

Cory Sexton, by the world's standards, was a man who had it all. He had the "Midas touch," and every business venture he attempted was extremely successful. Despite his financial prosperity, there was something significantly missing. His marriage was turbulent, and his children were losing their respect for their father, despite his business acumen.

Cory, like Jonah, had invested his income in things that took him on a trip that ever-increased his distance from God. Just as God awakened Jonah to his divine purpose, so God awakened Cory. In so doing, God saved his marriage and his children's respect. Today, Cory stands each week in the pulpit of Hoschton Baptist Church and helps others discover the life-changing principles of God's Word that radically altered his own life.

It is not surprising that Cory is passionate in helping Christians discover their purpose, renew their focus, and achieve true prosperity. Pastor Sexton's latest book, *Nine Concepts for the Christian from the Book of Jonah*, fulfills this passion. As you read this book, you will discover the heart of an evangelistic pastor who is eager to help other believers live above the level of mediocrity.

Prepare yourself to be convicted and corrected in areas where we all too often feel comfortable drifting away from God. The truths in this book are not merely academic. They are Biblically based and experientially proven by a pastor who has been there. Grab your Bible and prayerfully invest yourself in these "forty days" that just possibly could change the trajectory or your life.

Dr. Jeff Amsbaugh
Pensacola Christian College , Associate Teaching Professor
B.A., Tennessee Temple University
M.Div., Luther Rice Seminary
D.Min., Temple Baptist Seminary

Dedication

I would like to dedicate this effort …

To my God and my Savior, the Lord Jesus Christ who willingly humbled Himself. Left His throne in Glory. Took on the form of a servant and the likeness of men. And as a man humbled Himself by becoming obedient unto death, even the death of the cross. And this He did for me, as me, and in my place. And now I, knowing that He has died for me, seek to live for Him.

Also, to the love of my life, whom I met for the first time in 1983, at the tender youthful age of thirteen, and have loved ever since. She is my Butch Cassidy, she is my Doc Holiday, she is lovingly known as Sunshine and Dimples, and she is my person.

Karla, I Love You!

And to my children, Kayla, and Carter. Who always make me feel special and provide the courage for me to be me.

I also want to acknowledge the fine people of Hoschton Baptist Church who endure my preaching week in and week out, usually with a smile.

Lastly, special thanks to Amanda Crowe for her editorial efforts. She is a trooper and a friend.

9 Dependable Concepts Learned from Jonah

1. God calls every believer to serve, but not all are Compliant.

2. Every person is convicted of sin, but not all are Condemned.

3. Every Saint is Justified but not all are Just.

4. Every Disobedient Christian will be Disciplined.

5. The Natural Reflex of Repentance is Obedience.

6. Obedience Results in the Accomplishment of God's Will

7. When God sees Repentance. He Relents from Condemnation.

8. The Chief Desire of God for Man is Restoration.

9. The Restriction of Time. Today is the day for Repentance.

Table of Contents

Introduction

When you hear the name Jonah, used in a Christian or biblical context, what is the first thought that comes to your mind? A large fish? A battered vessel? A repentant King? A pouting prophet? If you are like me, it is a flannelgraph board and a big-haired teacher, named Ms. Eunice!

If you were a child, or if you simply raised children in the first part of the 21st century you may conjure an asparagus, a tomato, a cucumber, and the *"Pirates who don't do anything."* Either way, we habitually dismiss Jonah as a children's story, or as less than applicable to our Christian walk. After all, we are not sure about the fish, we do not see ourselves as prophets, we can't comprehend a savage people like the Ninevites, and we would never value a green gourd above that of human life.

Maybe you have heard Jonah used as an example for missions work, as an example of a missionary, or as an encouragement to go to the mission field, irrespective of the danger, believing that God has sent you and will therefore protect you (*even if it means nearly drowning, soaking in bleachy stomach acids for three days, being spit out by a large fish, looking like a bleached rag and smelling worse, in the end, only to find yourself suffering in the hot sun while pouting over the grace of God*). The exhortation would be to be faithful and obedient because you cannot run from God's calling on your life. But this exhortation carries an implied negative, such as "if you do not fulfill the call of God on your life, He will hunt you and haunt you into submission," which I do not find to be conducive to fruitful service to the Lord.

I propose that the Book of Jonah is for the covenant-bearing, born-again believer. While we may find many applicable concepts whereby to live our lives, as we observe Jonah's reactions and responses to God and his calling, the greatest value is observing God's reactions, responses, and restorative desires towards this wayward prophet. What is God's greatest desire for mankind? There are many, but one trumps them all. I hope you will follow me on this journey of discovery in The Story of Jonah.

"Jonah is unique in that it is more concerned with the Prophet than his prophecy. The condition of his soul, and God's loving discipline of him, instruct and humble the reader."
George Williams, founder of YMCA

Chapter One
Called, But Not Compliant

Jonah 1:1-3 Now the word of the Lord came unto Jonah the son of Amittai, saying, Arise, go to Nineveh, that great city, and cry against it; for their wickedness is come up before me. But Jonah rose up to flee unto Tarshish from the presence of the Lord and went down to Joppa; and he found a ship going to Tarshish: so, he paid the fare thereof, and went down into it, to go with them unto Tarshish from the presence of the Lord.

Before we note Jonah's response, let us consider the following question. Why is the book of Jonah in the Bible? This is a question that deserves consideration. Most other Old Testament books relate to Israel, but Jonah seems to stand alone. Even as we consider the book of Genesis, we see a book of beginnings, to include (eventually) the beginning of Israel. It is reasonable to say that the Pentateuch (*The First Five Books of the Bible*) establishes Israel, and then the Historical books detail her rise and fall (*Judges-Esther*). The Poetic books (*Job-Song of Solomon*) define her culture, and the Prophetical books (*Isaiah – Malachi*) describe her future; but what is the nature and purpose of the book of Jonah?

Jonah and its details provide us with brilliant details on the sovereignty of God. In it, we are reminded that He controls everything except the human will. Dr. Warren W. Wiersbe states, *"Everything in nature obeys God's Word except for Human Beings."* Jonah may also be seen as a clear typology or picture of the *Death, Burial, and Resurrection of Christ* as referenced by the Lord himself[1]. Furthermore, the events of Jonah are a valid warning to the Jews who heard Christ speak. The Son of God preached to the chosen nation of God for three years, centering on the Love of God and few repented. But Jonah, a rebellious prophet, preached one sermon to murderous gentiles concerning the wrath of God, and they all repented and were subsequently forgiven. The circumstances in Jonah teach that salvation is not by works; it is solely of the Lord. Jonah's rebellion shows that God's grace cannot be frustrated and that God will not cast a believer aside for faithlessness. He may sit you down, but when you are ready to serve in obedience, He will restore and use you. It reveals God's graciousness and goodness. It answers the Apostle Paul's question in Romans 3:29: "Is he the God of the Jews only? Is he not also of the Gentiles? Yes, He is God of the Gentiles also!"

Finally, we see that the man Jonah is a microcosm of the entire nation of Israel and the nation's past, present, and future. In his Bible Believers Commentary, William MacDonald lists the following observations. 1.) Israel was to be a witness for God to the Gentile nations. 2.) Jealous of the Grace of God, they refused to share His truth. 3.) Rebellious; cast into the sea (peoples/gentile nations), swallowed up but not assimilated by them. 4.) Future – Cast upon dry

---

[1] **Mathew 12:40** For as Jonas was three days and three nights in the whale's belly; so shall the Son of man be three days and three nights in the heart of the earth.

land and made a blessing to the nations. (*Israel restored in the Millennial Kingdom and blessing all nations.*)

This should give some comfort and comprehension concerning the validity and purpose of the book of Jonah. We will note as we process this book that the applications will deal with words and concepts like:

- Servanthood
- Calling
- Contradiction
- Revival
- Distraction
- Deliverance
- Conviction
- Displeasure
- Confessions
- Suffering
- Hope
- Salvation
- Running Away
- Evangelism
- Response
- Submission
- Contrasts
- Discipline
- Disobedience
- Devotion
- Condemnation
- Disappointment
- Repentance
- Mercy
- Grace
- Forgiveness
- Fear
- Standing Still
- Confusion

The first of the 9 Dependable Concepts from the Book of Jonah is:

1.   Every believer is called to serve, but not all are compliant.

I call your attention to the _Source of the Call_ in the first verse. It is simply _The Word of the LORD_. In today's culture and society, we receive a lot of information. We receive a lot of directions every day. We get information from news sources, podcasts, radio programming, and print material, all meant to subliminally influence our thinking. This is a fact; it occurs daily, and if you are not diligent with _your filter_ (as in _your control_ of what information you take in), you can become overwhelmed by a deluge of negativity and falsehood.

What does this "filter" look like? How does it work? Is it solely an issue of self-control? Is it an issue of quality? Or of quantity? Does it have a particular label? Is it branded? What is the proper blend of information? Is it a 50/50 of entertainment and self-help? How much news should I intake? How much vegging am I allowed? These questions have many answers, all couched in some form of dogma or belief structure. Without sounding like your pastor, priest, or parents, I want to insist that quality matters a great deal. And in the world of informational intake, there is no more excellent quality than the Word of God—the Bible. The 66 canonical books comprise one book of truth. Because of this, the sound encouragement is to be in the Word of God daily. It is inerrant, it is infallible, it is inspired, and it is eternal. Jonah heard directly from the Word of Jehovah. God spoke directly to him. There was no doubting the source or authenticity. And there is no reason to believe that Jonah doubted the source of the call.

This prompts the question: "Are you on good enough terms with God that He might just speak to you directly?" Before you answer, allow me to remind you that the Book of Hebrews tells us that in the past and in different times, God spoke to His servants through the prophets or a messenger. But now He speaks, not through a messenger, but God himself speaks through His son, the Lord Jesus Christ, because He is the express image and revelation of God. You might say that Christ is God's last and final word! The Gospel of John teaches that the Word became flesh and dwelt among us, and in his letter to the church at Corinth, the Apostle Paul would say of the Word of God *"When that which is perfect* (the completed Word of God) *is come, then that which is in part shall be done away."*

Allow me to rephrase the question: "Are you engaged in the Bible, the *Word of God,* enough for the God of the *Word* to speak to you? When He does, do you recognize the source of the Call as the Word of God?"

I am confident some will question whether God would call them, or me, or anyone. Doesn't the call only come to those who are special? Those who have a pedigree? Those who wear a hair shirt and stand on a pole? Those whom God has deemed worthy of a particular purpose? Well, let's consider the <u>*Servant who is Called*</u>. We note that the word of the Lord, *aka the call of God,* came unto <u>*Jonah, the son of Amittai*</u>. Who is Jonah? Is he a biblically historical person? What separates him from any other prophet from Gath-Hepher?

Jonah is somewhat obscure, but we know from 2 Kings that he did indeed exist, was a prophet, and was the son of Amittai. We also know that he was a historical bible character because the Lord Jesus Christ spoke of him concerning his (Christ's) own death, burial, and resurrection. But besides those two references and this short account, we know very little about Jonah. He was seemingly insignificant. You will find that true of many folks mentioned in the bible. They were only notable because God called them, spoke to them, touched them, redeemed them, or used them in some noteworthy way. What's important to understand is that Jonah *wasn't* exceptional. But he was called, and expected to obey. And I would remind you that according to the Great Commission, we are all called upon and expected to obey.

Every believer is called, but not all believers are compliant.

Now that we have established Jonah's "significant insignificance," let's consider the specific details of the call. It begins with an action component: "*Arise, go*." I love the specificity; it's brief and to the point. The entire call is immediate action: "Arise!" Doesn't that sound like Matthew 28:19 "Go ye"? The call continues with a geographical direction. "Go to Nineveh." We appreciate the direct nature of the call of God. There is no mystery or clue to decipher; the simple command is "*Go to Nineveh*." There is no guesswork, alternate explanation, or multiple choice. It's just direction. "Go to Nineveh!" We have similar instructions… We are to go into the World! Then, God gives Jonah a responsibility to perform: "*Cry Against it*." This is the fullness of the command. It is a direct order Jonah could not have misunderstood.

Later, when Jonah decides to obey God, his sermon for Nineveh consists of five words in the Hebrew language. This was a simple assignment, just as our assignment is simple. We are to be witnesses of Him, the one who loved us and died for us!

Regardless of how often I read Jonah's narrative and how well I understand mankind's disobedience toward God, I always feel a little unnerved by *the stubborn response to the* prophet's call. It has been stated that Jonah's response was willful and rebellious. Jonah was not merely *running* away or *resisting*, but rather, he was *resigning* his post and *retiring* from his position. Jonah was abandoning his responsibility.

If this statement is true of Jonah, what can be stated of the New Testament believer who willingly disregards or even unwittingly disrespects the Great Commission, the calls to separation and submission, or one of the other many implications of the written Word of God?

Every believer is Called but not all are Compliant.

Notice the details and actions associated with Jonah's reaction to God's call. Immediately, he decided to flee rather than to follow. Then, he traveled west rather than east. He fled away from the Lord's presence rather than towards it. His route carried him downward *(down to Joppa – down into the ship.)* And then, fleeing, he *willingly* paid the fare thereof. You will notice that all these things seem counterintuitive and antithetical to progress. This indicates resistance to the Word of the Lord, the Will of God, and the Walk of a Servant.

Now, we might speak of why Jonah resisted or refused. We could speak of fear, hate, or jealousy … but would any of it change the simple truth that Jonah acted in complete opposition to the command of the Lord?

The Short answer is "No." And that is the same answer you will give, regardless of any excuse, regret, or failure to comply. Disobedience to the Lord will be judged. Have you complied with the call of God in your life?

The first call in everyone's life is salvation: repent and believe the Gospel. "For God so loved the world, that he gave his only begotten

Son, that whosoever believeth in him should not perish, but have everlasting life." God's desire for your life is that you will be saved. He has paid your sin debt. He died for you, as you, and in your place. But you must respond in faith. It is not enough to believe that God is one; it is not enough to intellectually assent to the existence of a man named Jesus, or that He was crucified, or that He rose again. "If thou shalt confess with thy mouth the Lord Jesus, and believe in thine heart (faith) that God hath raised Him from the dead, thou shalt be saved!" If you are not a fan of the old English, hear it this way: "If you declare with your mouth, 'Jesus is Lord,' and believe in your heart that God raised him from the dead, you will be saved. For by grace are you saved through faith!"

Consider the second dependable concept that we can glean from this study.

2. Every person is convicted of sin, but not all are Condemned.

Indeed, we all stand convicted by the law of God. Because of this truth, the greatest needs in our lives are forgiveness and redemption. Romans 8:1 tells us that there is no condemnation to those who are in Christ Jesus.

Have you answered the call to salvation? To surrender? To submit? If so, then you are no longer under the condemnation of the law of God. You are now born-again and justified in the sight of God. You are a Saint of God, a Child of God, a Servant of the "Most High" God. But this is just the beginning of your journey; obedience is the first call in the believer's life. Are you obedient to the call of God in your life? *Remember, Every Servant is Called, but not all are Compliant.*

If you have never believed, would you consider these thoughts and pray, asking God to forgive you and to redeem you?

God, I realize that I am a sinner. I realize that you, through your precious son, have paid my sin debt. Lord, I am asking for your forgiveness today. Lord, I believe that you died for my sins, that you arose victorious over the death and the grave, and that you will one day return to receive your own unto yourself. Lord, I am asking you to redeem me and to become the Lord of my life. I am trusting in nothing but the grace of God for my pardon.

If you are born-again, you have been called to obedience.
Will you comply?

*"Let it never be forgotten that Jonah was a man of God.
I often hear great fault found with him, and he
richly deserves the condemnation; he was not at all an
amiable person; but, for all that, he was a man of God."*
Charles Spurgeon

Chapter Two
Called, But Not Answering

*Jonah 1:4-10 But the Lord sent out a great wind into the sea, and there
was a mighty tempest in the sea, so that the ship was like to be
broken. Then the mariners were afraid, and cried every man unto his
god, and cast forth the wares that were in the ship into the sea, to
lighten it of them. But Jonah was gone down into the sides of the ship;
and he lay and was fast asleep. So, the shipmaster came to him, and
said unto him, what meanest thou, O sleeper? arise, call upon thy God,
if so be that God will think upon us, that we perish not. And they said
everyone to his fellow, Come, and let us cast lots, that we may know
for whose cause this evil is upon us. So, they cast lots, and the lot fell
upon Jonah. Then said they unto him, Tell us, we pray thee, for whose
cause this evil is upon us; What is thine occupation? and whence
comest thou? What is thy country? and of what people art thou? And
he said unto them, I am an Hebrew; and I fear the Lord, the God of
heaven, which hath made the sea and the dry land. Then were the men
exceedingly afraid and said unto him. Why hast thou done this? For
the men knew that he fled from the presence of the Lord, because he
had told them.*

Almost immediately, Jonah's response is to retreat. As you consider the implications of this, ask yourself: are you advancing God's call, or retreating?

Notice how Jonah exhibits *the irrational behavior of the deserter*. He heard from God; he knows the source, but he chooses to flee rather than follow. In clarity, any time we choose to flee from the presence of God it is an irrational behavior because God is *omnipresent*, which simply means that we cannot flee from His presence because He is everywhere. This is one of several terms that refer to the essential qualities of God. The other common terms are *omnipotent*, which means "all-powerful," *omniscient*, which means "all-knowing," and *omni-benevolent*, which means "all-loving."

Interestingly enough, these characteristics are all reflected in Jonah's narrative. God knew where Jonah was, God used His power to toss the ship, and because of His omni-benevolence God preserved Jonah in the belly of the fish. The Psalmist concludes, "O Lord, you have searched me and known me! You know when I sit down and when I rise up; you discern my thoughts from afar. You search out my path and my lying down and are acquainted with all my ways. Even before a word is on my tongue, behold, O Lord, you know it altogether. You hem me in, behind and before, and lay your hand upon me. Such knowledge is too wonderful for me; it is high; I cannot attain it. Where shall I go from your Spirit? Or where shall I flee from your presence? If I ascend to heaven, you are there! If I make my bed in Sheol, you are there! If I take the wings of the morning and dwell in the uttermost parts of the sea, even there, your hand shall lead me, and your right hand shall hold me."[2] So, it is evident that we cannot escape God.

When we seek to retreat from His presence others will notice that, like Jonah, our *Conduct does not align with circumstances.* In his effort to retreat from God, Jonah goes to Joppa and finds a vessel with vacancy, pays the fare, and enters the ship. It appears that as soon as he boards the ship, he descends into the hull and quickly falls asleep. There he is, running for his life and away from God, and his best effort includes a nap. Even amid a storm, when the experienced mariners offload the wares of the ship to save the ship alive, Jonah is fast asleep. He does not respond correctly to the things going on around him.

We also see that his *confession does not align with his conduct*. As he becomes the center of attention because of his unconventional behavior, he confesses his relationship with the God of all Glory. Jonah says he fears the God of all creation, but instead of praying, he sleeps. If he fears the Creator, why doesn't he pray for the sake of the ship?

Lastly, Jonah's *character does not align with his calling*. He tells the mariners that he is a Hebrew, but he is running from the presence of the Lord. If he is a Hebrew, why is he fleeing his God? Why would he flee from the one in whom he believed? Not only is he a Hebrew who enjoys a covenant relationship with the one true God, but he is also a prophet who is especially gifted and specifically called. Do you realize that the very same is true for every born-again believer? Believers enjoy a covenant relationship with the God of Heaven, the King of

---

2 Psalm 139:1-10

Kings, and the Lord of Lords. Believers are specially gifted for a purpose in the body of Christ, aka the Church. Believers are specially called to be salt and light in this dark world.

Here we can introduce our third dependable concept.

3.   Every Saint is Justified but not all are Just.

This truth begs the question, how would your behavior as a believer be described? Does your conduct align with the circumstances of our society? Does your conduct betray your confession? Does your character align with your Christian calling?

Not only does Jonah display signs of irrationality, but he also portrays *indicative behaviors of the desperate*. Something I notice about myself, and many others in the church, is that often we are offended or at least caught off guard when lost folks act like … lost folks. When they are arrogant, dismissive of the gospel, self-centered, foul-mouthed, express a crude sense of humor, or even if they are sacrilegious, we can be contradictory, condemning, or even condescending. Knowing that they are lost and estranged from the Lord and His saving power, what should we expect? And much like the lost, these sailors respond to the crisis in the flesh.

The sailors' behavior exemplifies at least two common responses of desperate people. Due to the storm and likely some earlier life experience, the sailors *were afraid*. These were experienced sailors, but they were still scared. The power of the sea shook these men, and they responded in the only way they knew how. They fought the wind, forfeited their goods to the sea, and they sought the help of any god who might respond. In general, *they were and are searching for* _answers._ They cried out unto their gods and found no relief from the onslaught. Then, they found Jonah and asked him to pray to his God. They were not in the mood to debate; they were in a crisis and wanted help without warning or qualification. At this moment, they were willing to listen. These men did all they could do and came to an end of themselves…Have you been there?

Imagine if Jonah had been in the Will of God rather than running from it. What a fantastic opportunity of faith and trust could have been displayed here! But he was not. Even though he was out of step with the Lord's will, his testimony still carried some weight of validity as these sailors were convinced he was the answer and began seeking his instruction. We also have such an opportunity today; our testimony may be the light in someone's dark night. Our faithfulness may be the rock of hope that someone clings to when life's storms come. If we are faithful, obedient, and true, we can exert a lasting impact on people. I wonder how often we miss this same opportunity because we are asleep in the storm. Are you there for the needs and concerns of the desperate when the storms come? Are you surprised at the behavior of the lost? Is there something in your testimony that would draw the searchers to you?

I wonder if it seems to you, as it does to me, that Jonah is running in proverbial quicksand. As quickly and decisively as he fled, we would expect him to be further away. It is akin to a horror movie in which no one can escape the marauder, and the more they flee the more it seems he is right there. To some degree, this speaks to the "omni" characteristics of God. You remember God is all-powerful (omnipotent), ever-present (omnipresent), all-knowing (omniscient), and all-loving (omni-benevolent). It seems that God expresses these qualities in *the inhibiting behavior of the Deliverer.* Setting limits, designing protections, redirecting behaviors, interrupting progress, and simply allowing resistance – all to keep or take us where He intends for us to be.

These inhibiting behaviors apply to the born-again, the called, and the servant of God. Over and over, we see how *God takes part in our lives*, and these are measures of inhibition, restrictions, and limits that He institutes to guide us, even in our retreat. In fact, throughout the Scriptures, we see examples of God being intimately involved in the life of His chosen ones. It is evident from the very beginning. In Genesis, chapter 3, *God came seeking* that guilty pair. In Genesis chapter 12, in the life of Abram, *God called* a seemingly unaware man out of Ur of the Chaldees. In Genesis 19, *God retrieved* Lot and his family before destroying Sodom and Gomorrah. In Genesis chapter 28, *God reveals Himself* to Jacob at Bethel, and again in Genesis chapter 35. In Numbers chapter 22, the story of Balaam and the talking Donkey, *God intervenes* in another wayward prophet's life. In this case, with Jonah, we see that God sends several prepared things toward Jonah. He prepared the storm, the great fish, the gourd, the worm, and the vehement east wind. All these things would be used to redirect, correct, and employ Jonah in God's work for him.

The progression of events in Jonah's life is interesting. First, *God calls*. This call is clear. The Word of the Lord came unto Jonah. God called Jonah to his work and commissioned it to be done. It is quite easy to relate this to the commission and call given to all born-again believers. Next, *He Pursues*. After God calls Jonah, He follows him onto that ship and prepares the next instruction phase. Jonah was not allowed to run without resistance. He was not allowed to disappear, nor was he allowed to check out. Jonah was pursued by the call of God and the result was compliance.

I believe God works this way in the lives of His people, even today. I don't think we're allowed to escape the call without resistance. I believe He will pursue us. This is not to insinuate that God's grace is irresistible because it can be resisted. We can vex our righteous souls[3], and eventually be turned over to our vain imaginations, and our hearts can be darkened[4],. But the Lord is long-suffering and not willing that any should perish[5]. God wants what is best for His children.

He also Reveals. It's interesting and entertaining that the sailors knew Jonah was the problem, and how they perceived he had fled the presence of God. This is another aspect of God marking and revealing His own. You may feel as if you are hiding from the world, from your friends or foes … but often, they know before you do that God is working in your life. They know you belong to God, or that you have a higher purpose. Sometimes, the people around you may be suffering the consequences of your rebellion. Maybe they are enduring a storm because *you* are fleeing from God. Possibly, they are in danger of eternal condemnation because *you* are hiding from your responsibility to share the Gospel or be the light. This has happened more than once in my life, wherein God would use someone close to me or in my

---

[3] **2 Peter 2:8** (For that righteous man dwelling among them, in seeing and hearing, vexed his righteous soul from day to day with their unlawful deeds;)

[4] **Romans 1:21** Because that, when they knew God, they glorified him not as God, neither were thankful; but became vain in their imaginations, and their foolish heart was darkened.

[5] **2 Peter 3:9** The Lord is not slack concerning his promise, as some men count slackness; but is longsuffering to us-ward, not willing that any should perish, but that all should come to repentance.

general vicinity to speak to and encourage me to be who God called me to be! Rather than worrying about what some people think, why not just surrender to the Lord and accept who He says you are and what He has called you to do? Accept the responsibilities He has assigned you.

Have you ever fled from the presence of the Lord or the calling of God? Are you retreating even today? In what ways have you experienced the Lord inhibiting or limiting your progress? Have you been called to a ministry or a responsibility that you despise or detest? Who else is suffering for your disobedience?

The old hymn says, "I've wandered far away from God; now I am coming home." The prodigal son came to himself and determined he would rather be a servant in his father's house than a slave to the world. Rebellion doesn't make for a good life. What are you running from? How long will you retreat? Would you turn back to the Lord today?

Heavenly Father, I have been running from you, from your call, from your presence, and from my responsibility. Lord, forgive me. God, restore me. Lord, today I stop. Today, I comply. Today, I respond in obedience. Please calm the storm and give me the ability to fulfill your will.

Jonah is himself a strange paradox: a prophet of God, and yet a runaway from God: a man drowned, and yet alive: a preacher of repentance, yet one that repines at repentance.

A. R. Fausset

Chapter Three
Called, But Indifferent

Jonah 1:11-16 Then said they unto him, What shall we do unto thee, that the sea may be calm unto us? for the sea wrought, and was tempestuous. [12] *And he said unto them, Take me up, and cast me forth into the sea; so shall the sea be calm unto you: for I know that for my sake this great tempest is upon you.* [13] *Nevertheless the men rowed hard to bring it to the land; but they could not: for the sea wrought, and was tempestuous against them.* [14] *Wherefore they cried unto the Lord, and said, We beseech thee, O Lord, we beseech thee, let us not perish for this man's life, and lay not upon us innocent blood: for thou, O Lord, hast done as it pleased thee.* [15] *So they took up Jonah, and cast him forth into the sea: and the sea ceased from her raging.* [16] *Then the men feared the Lord exceedingly, and offered a sacrifice unto the Lord, and made vows.*

As a brief reminder, let's consider the dependable concepts that we have mentioned thus far.

1.   **God calls every believer to serve, but not all are Compliant.**

2.   **The law convicts every person of sin, but not all are Condemned.**

3. Every Saint is Justified but not all are Just.

We are now considering the third paragraph of the Book of Jonah. In the first paragraph, we noted Jonah's *Response* to God's call: to flee from God's presence. In the second paragraph, we examined how the response turned into a *Retreat* and discussed the retreat of the called. Next, we will see the literal *Resignation* of the Called.

As we study and work our way through this little book of the Old Testament, remember that beyond all the details of culture, character, dispensation, and reaction, there is a simplicity of truth: Jonah is a child of God, who receives a call from the *Word of God*, to go and fulfill the *Work of God*, according to the *Will of God*. In this sense, Jonah represents every born-again believer. You might say he is an "everyman …"

The plot of this specific historical event revolves around Jonah's responses. Thus far, he has chosen to resist, and fled. This flight is pictured as a retreat because it is in the opposite direction of advancing the will of God. We will see the full extent of his resistance in *his resignation*.

The seamen get caught unwittingly in Jonah's rebellious response and retreat. They are, up until this moment, completely unaware of who he is, who he belongs to, or what he has done. They likely found him odd, but the text only documents *the seamen's considerate response*. By the casting of lots and personal confession, they discovered that Jonah is the culprit. He is the cause of the storm, he knows the master of the storm, and he has brought the wrath of God upon all the inhabitants of the ship. Even though this is clear, they speak to him with compassion and respect concerning his position.

We can read the question (1:11), "What shall we do unto thee, that the sea may be calm unto us?" as an upsetting and antagonistic appeal, almost a shock that this guy has been so careless as to bring this calamity upon them. We see something similar when Abimelech discovers that Sarai is Abram's wife.[6] He says to Abram, incredulously, "What hast thou done to us?" Fearing God's judgment, he responds in a similar tone.

The seamen are afraid because they are aware Jonah has fled from a very powerful god, and seemingly upset the creator of all (1:9). But they are also fearful in a reverential way as they ask, "What can be done to calm the sea?" They realize that Jonah has the answer, and (above all else) the relationship to resolve the situation.

Again, there are two points of consideration and application for us here. The first speaks to *accountability*, and the second speaks to *responsibility*. Jonah's disobedience brought the wrath of God upon these men. There is a similarity with the account of Abimelech and Abram because God warned Abram not to depart from the land. Abram disobeyed and set in motion the events of **Genesis 20,** which ultimately brought a curse upon the house of Abimelech. There is an NT event that is similar, wherein the first church was told to go out into all the surrounding region, and when they did not it brought about persecution. When we resist evangelizing and refuse to be witnesses

---

6 **Genesis 20:9-10** Then Abimelech called Abraham, and said unto him, What hast thou done unto us? and what have I offended thee, that thou hast brought on me and on my kingdom a great sin? thou hast done deeds unto me that ought not to be done.[10] And Abimelech said unto Abraham, What sawest thou, that thou hast done this thing?

unto God, who will suffer the most? The disobedient child of God, or the unregenerate child of the world?

Then there is the issue of *Responsibility*. When lost souls seek relief from suffering, are you prepared to give them a viable answer? Which is Faith alone, in Christ alone! We know that even in Jonah's dilapidated state, stemming from his rebellion, he is still the source of the answer in this time of trouble. You may run from your calling, resist your creator, hide and try to sleep through the troubles of life, but you are still a child of God. There is still a regenerated spirit within you, and you are still accountable to your calling and responsible to the spiritual needs of those around you.

In stark contrast to the mariner's compassion, we are struck by *the callous resignation of the prophet*. The drama doesn't bother Jonah; he seems unfazed by his resistance and retreat.

Perhaps you know the adage, "You've made your bed; now you will have to lie in it!" This speaks to the consequences of our actions and decisions. Sometimes, there is no way out but to face them. We must endure the difficulties. Jonah seems to embrace that mentality here. He seems to say, "I have made my bed, and now I will just lie in it!" In other words, "*I will not relent, I will not repent, I will not comply, I would rather die.*"

God is the righteous judge of all the earth, and therefore He will always do right.[7] In judgment, God will remember mercy.[8] And when we are wrong, we may repent, and when we repent, He will forgive us and restore us.[9] I would expect Jonah, a prophet of God, to know and embrace this truth. But he is stuck at "*I will not relent, I will not repent, I will not comply, I would rather die.*"

We might feel that Jonah exhibits some compassion, or worries for the sailors' wellbeing. Maybe he believed that he should sacrifice himself, for the good of the vessel and all who were on board. But he is also a prophet of the Most High God, the Creator of all, the Master of the Universe, the omnipotent, omniscient, omnipresent, and omni-benevolent God. Jonah could simply pray and ask God to calm the seas.

I prefer to call your attention to *two other details* that may be less obvious.

The first is that Jonah is simply *unwilling* to repent to God; he would prefer to die rather than comply. This eclipses stubbornness, surpasses hardheadedness, and is worse than selfishness. It is the attitude of a petulant child. It is the inability to consider the greater good, to see the big picture, or to comprehend the victory. This is not an *uncommon* human reaction, but it is *unbecoming* a Child of God.

---

[7] **Genesis 18:25** That be far from thee to do after this manner, to slay the righteous with the wicked: and that the righteous should be as the wicked, that be far from thee: Shall not the Judge of all the earth do right?

[8] **Habakkuk 3:2** O Lord, I have heard thy speech, and was afraid: O Lord, revive thy work in the midst of the years, in the midst of the years make known; in wrath remember mercy.

[9] **1 John 1:9** If we confess our sins, he is faithful and just to forgive us our sins, and to cleanse us from all unrighteousness.

Secondly, I want you to consider his false piety even in retreat. Have you ever considered why he asked them to throw him overboard? If indeed, he could stop the storm, and save the seamen, why didn't he just cast himself into the sea? Dive right in and stop the storm! Why must he implicate them in his demise? Well, in my opinion, it was another aspect of victimhood. If he threw himself over, he would be known as a suicide, a coward, someone unwilling to endure difficulty. But, if he was thrown overboard, he would suddenly become a hero, a victim of cruelty, and maybe even a martyr. And best of all he was not guilty of suicide, which was against rabbinical law. Even this is a form of a lie. The motivation of Jonah's heart is the same. The fact is Jonah simply wanted to resign. He wanted to be thrown overboard and die.

For consideration, I would like to point you to believers who have experienced some form of church hurt, preacher hurt, or other emotional/spiritual injuries. People who become calloused to the call of God or their need for connection to the body of Christ. The ones who can tell you everything they have done in one breath, and all that they are unwilling to do in the next. These folks have resigned. They're determined to be "dead" to the church, specifically through active involvement in the local assembly. They demonstrate a surface level of piety, made completely false by their non-participation in the body-work of the church. They play the victim, seeking a martyr's title. But I believe they fail the world around them – friends, spouses, and children. How can you witness to the glory and honor of God if you refuse to obey His most basic commands?

In the moments following Jonah's callous retort, we are again impressed with *the courageous reaction of the workmen*. Acting more like saints than sailors, these men attempted with all their ability to bring the ship to shore. "*Attempted to row hard*" implies digging in the sea. They worked feverishly, making their greatest effort to keep from throwing Jonah into the sea. They tried to right the ship, on their own, and spare the rebellious prophet, but they could not. Their efforts were vigorous and well-intentioned, but they were faulty and in vain. There was only one way that they could be saved alive, without throwing Jonah into the water. No amount of work could overcome the raging sea.

Today, many well-intentioned folks try hard to bring their ships to shore. They seek the Peace of God, but it is only found in the person of Jesus Christ. As the Ambassadors of Christ, let us arise and show them the way! As it relates to salvation, forgiveness, remission of sin, redemption of the lost, and regeneration of the dead, the only hope is found in the finished work of Christ at Calvary. We cannot earn it, and we cannot buy it, we can only receive it by faith.

Next, we hear the seamen _cry for a reprieve of guilt_. These same men were previously (v.5) crying out, "each man to his own god." Now these polytheistic gentiles focus on the one true God, and in a moment of distress they begin to call upon Him, the one they believe can make a difference. Immediately, they ask for forgiveness for the shedding of innocent blood. And then, in a moment of _faith, belief,_ and _obedience_, they cast Jonah into the sea, and the sea ceased from its rage. How often do we wait until we are in terrible distress before calling upon the name of the Lord? All too often…

Though this was hardly a salvific moment for these sailors, pay attention to the **typology of this moment**. They prayed to the one true God, asking for forgiveness. They acted in faith, throwing Jonah overboard and believing this would appease God. And so, they were obedient to the instruction. In this moment, Jonah becomes a type of Christ, the object of their faith. He becomes the substitute. The way to peace with God. The protection against the wrath of God. All that Jonah does is suspect, but in type and representation, he resembles Christ satisfying the wrath of God on our behalf.

Have you come to this place of *faith*, *belief*, and *obedience*? Have you *realized* that the wrath of God is upon you? Have you *comprehended* that there is no God but Him? Have you given up all the other gods who cannot deliver you? Dead works, wealth, happiness, love of man, success, notoriety, pride? Have you *recognized* that Christ died for you, as you, in your place? The innocent for the guilty? Have you Trusted? Have you Repented? Have you Believed?

Also, notice the behavior of the sailors after the waves cease. It reminds me of *the communion of the redeemed*. These sailors are now acting like saints. They are fearing the Lord and offering sacrifices, or at least vows of sacrifices to come. They are experiencing and enjoying the calm seas of peace with God. Isn't that what you truly want? Don't we all desire to be at peace with God? Enjoying the Communion of the Redeemed? It could be yours today. Just repent of your unbelief. Christ died for you. Confess Him as Lord of your life and enjoy peace today.

There are two identities to acknowledge at this moment. Maybe you are the sailor in need of redemption. Or, possibly you are the prodigal prophet in need of restoration. Are you willing to martyr yourself on the altar of autonomy? Or will you repent and obey God's will for your life?

Father, we come now in prayer as we are, where we are, who we are, seeking you! Lord, would you reveal to us our greatest need? For the one in need of salvation, I pray for understanding. Clearly reveal yourself, Lord, show them their need, and quicken their dead spirit. For the wayward servant, Lord, I pray for their obedience. Help them choose you in this moment.

"Men say, 'Well, you don't believe in the story of Jonah and the whale, do you?' I want to tell you I do believe it. Christ did not doubt the story. He said His resurrection would be a sign like that given unto the Ninevites. It was the resurrected man Jonah who walked through the streets of Nineveh. They say a whale's throat is no larger than a man's fist, and it is physically impossible for a whale to swallow a man. The book of Jonah says that God prepared a great fish to swallow Jonah. Couldn't God make a fish large enough to swallow Jonah? If God could create a world, I think He could create a fish large enough to swallow a million men."

D. L. Moody, concerning Jonah and the great fish.

Chapter Four
Called and Corrected

Jonah 1:17-2:9 Now the Lord had prepared a great fish to swallow up Jonah. And Jonah was in the belly of the fish three days and three nights. Then Jonah prayed unto the Lord his God out of the fish's belly. And said, I cried by reason of mine affliction unto the Lord, and he heard me; out of the belly of hell cried I, and thou heardest my voice. For thou hadst cast me into the deep, in the midst of the seas; and the floods compassed me about: all thy billows and thy waves passed over me. Then I said, I am cast out of thy sight; yet I will look again toward thy holy temple.5 The waters compassed me about, even to the soul: the depth closed me round about, the weeds were wrapped about my head. I went down to the bottoms of the mountains; the earth with her bars was about me forever: yet hast thou brought up my life from corruption, O Lord my God. When my soul fainted within me I remembered the Lord: and my prayer came in unto thee, into thine holy temple. They that observe lying vanities forsake their own mercy. But I will sacrifice unto thee with the voice of thanksgiving; I will pay that that I have vowed. Salvation is of the Lord.

In the fourth paragraph of our experience with Jonah lies the proverbial "coming to the end of ourselves" moment. Many of us have experienced this, some more than others, and several of us are likely due for another one.

We discussed the ugly response that led to a retreat, concluding in the resignation of God's chosen servant. We have spoken of the historical implications, as well as some of the prophetic implications of Israel as God's chosen nation, unwilling to obey due to pride, and withholding the blessing they were intended to be to Gentile nations.

Also noted were applications to today's church: not fully obeying God's call to "Go" – the individual obligations of the believer to be witnesses unto Him among all peoples. At times, we all have responded poorly to God's call and command, possibly even retreated. We have all felt like resigning. We all know someone who refused to re-enlist.

The first of our dependable concepts tells us that all of God's children, (*born-again believers*), are called but not all are compliant. A subsequent truth to consider is God will not cast a believer aside, (as to destruction, or disposal), for faithlessness. He may sit you down, but when you are ready to serve in obedience, He can restore and use you. This points to our fourth dependable concept.

4. Every Disobedient Christian will be Disciplined.

While it is certain that every disobedient child of God will be disciplined,[10] not all disciplined children are restored. The process of restoration is often accompanied by some form of discipline or chastisement and always requires repentance.

If you were raised around Atlanta in the 1970s and 80s you may remember this announcement, with some nostalgia. *"We have arrived at a great moment in time!"* The rest of that announcement used to say it's Friday, it's Friday, it's Friday! This was the five o'clock announcement that aired every Friday on WKLS-96 Rock. That announcement used to provide me with an unfettered excitement for the weekend. I am happy to say, "We have arrived at a great time! It's Fish Day, it's Fish Day, it's Fish Day!" We are finally allowed to meet God's method of retribution, reinforcement, redirection, and eventually repentance for Jonah!

The _great fish was prepared and preemptive_. There are several "Prepared" things in the Book of Jonah. The *Great Storm*, the *Great Fish*, the *Gourd*, the *Worm,* and the *Vehement East Wind.* God prepared each of these things for Jonah, and they led to one or more of the following: _discipline to the prophet, direction for the prophet, development of the prophet,_ or the _demonstration of the power of God._ Each is intended to challenge Jonah, and in the _challenge_, the goal is _conviction_ and _conversion._ In my opinion, we can see events like these in our lives, and in each, we can witness the *Hand of God* moving.

Some write these events off as *good luck, bad luck, fortune,* or *folly.* But the believer should understand that *"all things work together for*

---

[10] **Hebrews 12:6** For whom the Lord loveth he chasteneth, and scourgeth every son whom he receiveth.

good to them that love God, to them who are the called according to His purpose."[11]

God is Sovereign, and all things happen for a reason. This is true of all of life. God is directing events around us, and I believe every event is for *direction, development, discipline,* or *demonstration*. Though I cannot explain exactly how and why this works, or answer some of the questions this truth will elicit, I believe these events are preemptive and/or anticipatory of my actions (which God knows ahead of time), and corrective. I know as a believer that if I observe the things, events, people, and moments God brings into my life, I will never be at a loss for *growth, guidance,* or *good insight*.

The great fish provided preserving and protective *discipline*. It was an alternative to drowning. I am not in a hurry to be swallowed by a large fish, but if I were sinking into the depths of the sea, drowning, without hope of survival, and a great fish swallowed me, the fish might improve the immediate circumstance. Either I am dead and no longer drowning, or else I am inside the fish and able to breathe.

Theologians have argued for eons as to whether Jonah sank and died and then was swallowed, or if he was swallowed and then died, or if he was swallowed and lived for those three days inside the fish. I'm not sure it matters; three days later, Jonah was walking and talking and headed towards the original destination of Nineveh. This helps us see the corrective value of this specific disciplinary action. The fish was never intended for destruction. Rather it was for *direction, discipline,* and *development*. The fish resulted in a "preserved" Jonah. If he had

---

[11] **Romans 8:28** And we know that all things work together for good to them that love God, to them who are the called according to his purpose.

been left to the sea, he would have drowned, but he was not left to the sea because God is sovereign, and He is always at work in the lives of His children.

Metaphorically speaking, if you are drowning in the sea of bad decisions, and God swallows you up in discipline, do not give up – look up and repent! He is working for your good and His Glory!

Another aspect of this narrative section is _the precise and prophetic time_. I appreciate that the time was precise. Indeed, the time was prophetic, as Christ mentions it concerning His time of death, burial, and resurrection. The applicable lesson for us is that God determined the length of the discipline. And it was just as long as it took for repentance to occur. Again, this speaks to the truth that _God will not cast a believer aside for faithlessness. He may sit you down, but when you are ready to serve in obedience, He will restore and use you._ He will not forget, overlook, discard, or permanently disqualify you. He is just looking for repentance or acquiescence. 1 John 1:9 speaks of confession: "_If we confess our sins, he is faithful and just to forgive our sins, and to cleanse us from all unrighteousness._" The operative word is "_confess_"; the Greek word is _homologia_, and it means "same words" or "to say the same words."

We must see our sin as God sees our sin. We must say the same thing about our sins as He says about them. This is, indeed, what God wants: for you to agree with Him about the wickedness of your sin and the righteousness of His Son. About the penalty of your sin, and the propitiation of His Son! "Propitiation" is a biblical word that simply means appeasement or atonement, and it speaks of the satisfaction of the wrath of God on your behalf, which was wrought by Christ on the cross. Because of His sacrifice, you may experience atonement, meaning you are set *at one* again with the Father. When you repent of your sinfulness, He will relent in His condemnation. He will see you in the righteousness of His Son, the Lord Jesus Christ. For the Born-again believer, when you relent of your disobedience, He will restore you to service and usefulness.

Jonah 2:1-9 is a prayer. This prayer shows us *the result of the discipline was repentance and promise*. All these verses contain the prayer of Jonah that modeled repentance and resulted in a pledge to keep his vow. Below is a list of acknowledgments and actions that are evident in this prayer.

- Vs. 2 Jonah Acknowledges God's Hearing – He Heard me!
- Vs. 3 Jonah Acknowledges God's Hand – He Had me!
- Vs. 4 Jonah Acknowledges God's Holiness – His Holy Temple!
- Vs. 5-7 Jonah Acknowledges God's Help – He brought me Life!
- Vs. 8 Jonah Repents – His Sin!
- Vs. 9 Jonah Commits to Follow – *I Will Pay! I have Vowed!* His Actions!

This is a good model for prayer. We all have a similar need for repentance and acknowledgment at times in our lives. I want to encourage the reader: no matter who you are, where you are, what you are doing, what you have done, what you are guilty of, what you are ashamed of … if you are running or hiding, if you've been arrogant or hateful, it doesn't matter. If you seek God in repentance, He will Hear you! He has His hand on you. He is Holy and thus will do right. And He will Help you! Will you be obedient?

If you are backslidden, He will forgive and restore you to righteousness. If you are unregenerate, He will give you "new life" and seal you until the Day of Redemption. You need only to Repent! And He will do the rest. Every event is for direction, development, discipline, or demonstration!

Would you pray?

Heavenly Father, please forgive me, heal me, cleanse me, deliver me, Lord, please restore me! I freely acknowledge your holiness, and my wickedness, and trust your hand! Amen

" 'And the Lord spake unto the fish, and it vomited out Jonah upon the dry land.' Sometimes, we don't have much choice about how we will be delivered. Jonah might have preferred another method, but God had a purpose in this also."
David Guzik

Chapter Five
Called and Restored

Jonah 2:10-3:4 And the Lord spake unto the fish, and it vomited out Jonah upon the dry land. And the word of the Lord came unto Jonah the second time, saying Arise, go unto Nineveh, that great city, and preach unto it the preaching that I bid thee. So, Jonah arose, and went unto Nineveh, according to the word of the Lord. Now Nineveh was an exceeding great city of three days' journey. And Jonah began to enter into the city a day's journey, and he cried, and said, yet forty days, and Nineveh shall be overthrown.

As we closed the last chapter, we considered the result of Jonah's disobedience, which was a prayer of repentance in chapter 2:1-9. We also noted the *Response of God*. We understand that God *heard* the call, He *held* the penitent in his hand, He is *Holy* (an immutable characteristic), and lastly, He *helped* by restoring Jonah's life.

We have thus far established four dependable concepts.

1. **God calls every believer to serve, but not all are Compliant.**
2. **The law convicts every person of sin, but not all are Condemned.**

3.   **Every Saint is Justified but not all are Just.**

4.   **Every Disobedient Christian will be Disciplined.**

In this chapter covering the next five verses of Jonah's narrative, we will seek to establish a fifth dependable concept.

5.   **The Natural Reflex of Repentance is Obedience.**

First, we should note that _repentance allows for restoration_. Jonah's _restoration was immediate and complete but likely marked him for life_. If we consider the Scripture chronologically, we see Jonah's repentance in verses 8-9, along with the representative truth that Salvation is of the Lord!

Repentance is ushered in by reality; the reality is that God is Sovereign, and if Sovereign is certainly in control. This is the reality that precedes the representative truth spoken by Jonah. Salvation is of the Lord. I hope that you realize this today. Salvation is not of works, education, knowledge, wisdom, sacrifice, membership, or any other accomplishment of man. Salvation is of the Lord. It is a gift that has been proffered unto you, which was purchased by God and accomplished by His Son, The Lord Jesus Christ, who is "The" (definite article! – one and only) mediator between man and God![12] _As soon as this Repentance was recorded, the Lord spoke, and the Fish spat!_ In every situation we see in the scripture, repentance is followed by restoration.

---

[12] **1 Timothy 2:5** For there is one God, and one mediator between God and men, the man Christ Jesus;

When the children of Israel repented, they were restored under the protective arm of God. Consider *Judges 2:16-18, 3:9, 3:15, 4:3,*[13] trust me it is redundantly true. When David repented of his sin with Bathsheba, he was restored to righteousness with God,[14] . Time and again, restoration follows repentance. If we believe that God works through difficulties in our life with a mind to *discipline, direct, develop,* or *demonstrate* to us His power, goodness, love, mercy, grace, or sovereignty … then we must also believe that He seeks our agreement. Usually, it takes the form of a repentant action, which God uses to *Restore* us.

Indeed, this is the case with Jonah. He was restored, placed on dry land, on his own two feet, and given the opportunity to obey. However, we should consider the marks left on the disobedient prophet.

---

[13] **Judges 2:16-18** Nevertheless the Lord raised up judges, which delivered them out of the hand of those that spoiled them.[17] And yet they would not hearken unto their judges, but they went a whoring after other gods, and bowed themselves unto them: they turned quickly out of the way which their fathers walked in, obeying the commandments of the Lord; but they did not so.[18] And when the Lord raised them up judges, then the Lord was with the judge, and delivered them out of the hand of their enemies all the days of the judge: for it repented the Lord because of their groanings by reason of them that oppressed them and vexed them.

Judges 3:9 And when the children of Israel cried unto the Lord, the Lord raised up a deliverer to the children of Israel, who delivered them, even Othniel the son of Kenaz, Caleb's younger brother.

Judges 3:15 But when the children of Israel cried unto the Lord, the Lord raised them up a deliverer, Ehud the son of Gera, a Benjamite, a man lefthanded: and by him the children of Israel sent a present unto Eglon the king of Moab.

Judges 4:3 And the children of Israel cried unto the Lord: for he had nine hundred chariots of iron; and twenty years he mightily oppressed the children of Israel.

[14] **Psalm 51**

Is it reasonable to believe that Jonah had no signs of damage or residue of rebellion? Didn't Jacob walk with a limp after he wrestled with God?[15] Didn't David have disunity and sexual immorality in his household?[16] [17] Surely, we can see that sin leaves a scar, and rebellion is a sin. We can imagine how Jonah looked after floating in the digestive juices of the great fish for three days. I believe the marks and signs may have given him power among the Ninevites, who worshiped the fish god!

If we aren't careful, we can become overwhelmed by our own inadequacies, handicaps, and scars of sin and rebellion in our lives. Those scars should not disqualify or disable; rather they are distinguishing degrees of experience. Repentance brings restoration. There may be scars, and there may be marks, but they are only reminders that empower and enable us to remain true to the calling.

Next, we understand that _restoration assumes responsibility_ (3:1-2). This may be a new responsibility, but for Jonah, it is a _renewed responsibility_. You might even call it a _recommissioning_. The message didn't change, and neither did the call. Only the man changed.

Restored and standing on the dry land, likely back where he started, and in right relationship with the Lord, God's call comes again. _Remember, God will not permanently disqualify a believer for failures of faithlessness. "The Word of the Lord said go to Nineveh and preach_

---

[15] **Genesis 32:31** And as he passed over Penuel the sun rose upon him, and he halted upon his thigh.

[16] **2 Samuel 13**

[17] **2 Samuel 15**

the preaching I bid thee (KJV). Proclaim to it the proclamation that I share with you (NASB). Call out against it the message that I tell you (ESV)." The message, mission, motivation, and destination are all the same.

Jonah did not escape the calling, the storm, the fish, or the responsibility! Repentance removes the blight of condemnation, but the burden of the call remains! We're called according to His purpose.[18] We are called to be salt and light,[19] to be witnesses unto Him,[20] to occupy ourselves until He comes,[21] to study and preach the Word,[22] and to be approved Workmen,[23] to walk worthy of the name of

---

[18] **Ephesians 4:1** I therefore, the prisoner of the Lord, beseech you that ye walk worthy of the vocation wherewith ye are called,

[19] **Matthew 5:13-16** Ye are the salt of the earth: but if the salt have lost his savor, wherewith shall it be salted? it is thenceforth good for nothing, but to be cast out, and to be trodden under foot of men.
[14] Ye are the light of the world. A city that is set on an hill cannot be hid.[15] Neither do men light a candle, and put it under a bushel, but on a candlestick; and it giveth light unto all that are in the house.[16] Let your light so shine before men, that they may see your good works, and glorify your Father which is in heaven.

[20] **Acts 1:8** But ye shall receive power, after that the Holy Ghost is come upon you: and ye shall be witnesses unto me both in Jerusalem, and in all Judaea, and in Samaria, and unto the uttermost part of the earth.

[21] **Luke 19:13** And he called his ten servants, and delivered them ten pounds, and said unto them, Occupy till I come.

[22] **2 Timothy 4:2** Preach the word; be instant in season, out of season; reprove, rebuke, exhort with all long suffering and doctrine.

[23] **2 Timothy 2:15** Study to shew thyself approved unto God, a workman that needeth not to be ashamed, rightly dividing the word of truth.

Christ,[24] to be the body,[25] to not forsake the assembling of ourselves together,[26] to love the Lord God with all of our hearts, our soul, and our minds,[27] and to love our neighbors as ourselves.[28]

When we repent, we acknowledge these responsibilities: not unto salvation, but from salvation; not for victory, but from victory; not for forgiveness, but from a position of forgiveness. *Repentance allows Restoration, and Restoration assumes Responsibility…*

Lastly, *responsibility anticipates obedience* (3:3-4). The key word for me in this passage is the first word of verse three. I am less than well-developed in grammar, English or otherwise, but I looked at this word and discovered that it is a *Subordinating Conjunction* (which means connector), both in English and the Aramaic language. It is a *Copulative Conjunction,* which also simply means "connector." But in the Hebrew language it possesses a *Demonstrative Force.* This means that it isn't just connecting the actions of Jonah to all that has gone

---

[24] **Ephesians 4:1** I therefore, the prisoner of the Lord, beseech you that ye walk worthy of the vocation wherewith ye are called,

[25] **1 Corinthians 12:12-14** For as the body is one, and hath many members, and all the members of that one body, being many, are one body: so also is Christ.[13] For by one Spirit are we all baptized into one body, whether we be Jews or Gentiles, whether we be bond or free; and have been all made to drink into one Spirit.[14] For the body is not one member, but many.

[26] **Hebrews 10:25** Not forsaking the assembling of ourselves together, as the manner of some is; but exhorting one another: and so much the more, as ye see the day approaching.

[27] **Mark 12:30** And thou shalt love the Lord thy God with all thy heart, and with all thy soul, and with all thy mind, and with all thy strength: this is the first commandment.

[28] **James 2:8** If ye fulfil the royal law according to the scripture, Thou shalt love thy neighbour as thyself, ye do well:

before, but it suggests that his actions were expected as if this is the natural order of events. The only details that had changed were Jonah's *actions*, *attitude*, and *aims*.

Notice the juxtaposition in 1:3 and 3:3. First, Jonah arose to flee; now, he arose and went according to the word of the Lord, and once he arrived, he cried against the city. After his repentance, Jonah determines to be obedient despite his personal feelings about the Ninevites and the mission *because the Natural Reflex of Repentance is Obedience!* The antithesis of obedience is disobedience. The rehabilitation of disobedience is repentance; repentance from disobedience is obedience.

The natural reflex of repentance is obedience!

Would you define yourself as "resistant," or "receptive" to the call of God? Do you love the Lord with your whole person? Do you actively seek to fulfill the Great Commission, witnessing unto the Lord Jesus Christ everywhere you go? Is there a need for repentance or restoration in your life? Are you fulfilling your responsibilities unto the Lord? Have you been obedient unto the call for *salvation? Restoration? Action?*

"Father, we come to you now in complete honesty. We have all failed in some aspect of obedience. We find ourselves in need of restoration through repentance. We ask you now to challenge, charge, convict, convert, and Lord restore unto us the joy of Your salvation, of obedience unto you, the glory of serving you, and the peace that comes from our repentance.

"Jonah is the best illustration in the Bible of what a missionary should not do. He is disobedient, selfish, sinful; he has a rotten disposition. He is prejudiced. And yet the Lord puts his story here because it is so instructive. He teaches us more about the wrong way to do things than anyone called of God to a specific task. It's a marvelous lesson we learn from Jonah."

John MacArthur

Chapter Six
Called and Rewarded

Jonah 3:5-9 So the people of Nineveh believed God, and proclaimed a fast, and put on sackcloth, from the greatest of them even to the least of them. For word came unto the king of Nineveh, and he arose from his throne, and he laid his robe from him, and covered him with sackcloth, and sat in ashes. And he caused it to be proclaimed and published through Nineveh by the decree of the king and his nobles, saying, Let neither man nor beast, herd nor flock, taste anything: let them not feed, nor drink water: But let man and beast be covered with sackcloth, and cry mightily unto God: yea, let them turn everyone from his evil way, and from the violence that is in their hands. Who can tell if God will turn and repent, and turn away from his fierce anger, that we perish not?

We have considered five paragraphs of Jonah's story. In the first paragraph, Jonah Responds to the call of God; in the second, he Retreats; in the third, he Resigns; in the fourth, he Repents; and in the fifth, he is Restored. We have already discussed the result of Jonah's restoration. It was immediate and complete. It came equipped with a renewed commission or an assumed responsibility, and it anticipated compliance because *the natural reflex of repentance is obedience.* We have thus far established five dependable concepts. In these next few verses, we will establish a sixth.

6. Obedience Results in the accomplishment of God's Will

Obedience is key in the economy of God. Isaiah 55:11 states, *"God's Word will not return void but will prosper and accomplish the task unto which it is sent."* The Lord spoke to King Saul's disobedience by the prophet Samuel: *"Hath the Lord as great delight in burnt offerings and sacrifices, as in obeying the voice of the Lord? Behold, to obey is better than sacrifice, and to hearken than the fat of rams."*[29] Obedience is better than sacrifice. Peter told the Sanhedrin, *"We must obey God rather than men."*[30] The Lord asks us all, *"Why do you call me Lord, Lord, and not do what I tell you?"*[31] It is clear that the Sovereign, omnipotent, omniscient, omnipresent, and omni-benevolent God of the Universe is seeking obedience, and it is also clear that when we obey the word of God, we will see the will of God fulfilled.

The most common defense for Jonah's behavior revolves around the people he was called to reach. Typically, we speak of the "bad blood" between the Jews and the Ninevites or the Ninevites' cruel, inhumane

---

[29] **1 Samuel 15:22** And Samuel said, Hath the Lord as great delight in burnt offerings and sacrifices, as in obeying the voice of the Lord? Behold, to obey is better than sacrifice, and to hearken than the fat of rams.

[30] **Acts 5:29** Then Peter and the other apostles answered and said, We ought to obey God rather than men.

[31] **Luke 6:46** And why call ye me, Lord, Lord, and do not the things which I say?

nature. While this is not a valid excuse, I want you to understand a little about the people Jonah is preaching to.

Nineveh and its inhabitants were of the most wicked sort. It is known in history as the "Bloody City." It is first noted as a city founded by Nimrod, who was himself opposed to Jehovah and the roots of this place are well established in his insolent hatred of God.

According to John MacArthur, "It was a city of approximately 600,000 people according to archeology. It was located on the east bank of the Tigris River. It was very advanced culturally. The people were arrogant; they were proud of their achievements, but it was sinking in corruption. Nahum, the prophet who also spoke against Nineveh, called it a bloody city full of fraud, full of lies, full of robbery, full of sensuousness, full of violence, witchcraft, and idolatry. Their soldiers were famous around the world for brutality and cruelty. And God knew very well about their wickedness."

Notice also these two passages of historical effect, both taken from an article in the Christian Publishing House:

"I built a pillar over against his city gate, and I flayed all the chief men who had revolted, and I covered the pillar with their skins; some I walled up within the pillar, some I impaled upon the pillar on stakes, and I cut off the limbs of the officers, of the royal officers who had rebelled. Many captives from among them I burned with fire, and many I took as living captives. From some I cut off their hands and their fingers, and from others, I cut off their noses, their ears, and their fingers, of many I put out the eyes. I made one pillar of the living, and another of heads, and I bound their heads to posts (tree trunks) round

about the city. Their young men and maidens I burned in the fire . . . Twenty men I captured alive, and I immured them in the wall of his palace. The rest of them [their warriors] I consumed with thirst in the desert of the Euphrates." - The Words of a Ninevite King

"As the Assyrian army arrived back to Nineveh from a successful campaign, its captives were well aware of the horrors that awaited them, for they were in for unthinkable suffering and cruelty. As the soldiers came over the horizon, there would be numerous lines of captives, being led by cords that had hooks, which were pierced through the nose or lips. Many could look forward to being blinded by the King of Nineveh himself, who would use the point of a spear. Other prisoners awaited impalement, being hanged by their nude bodies upon pointed stakes that were run up through the stomachs into the chest cavities of the victims. Others still were whipped or beaten severely and then had their skin removed from their body while still alive. It is this fear factor that made Nineveh the great military machine that would march on another city, and its inhabitants would surrender without a fight." - The words of a Historian.

Lastly the passage from *Nahum* 3:1-7: *Woe to the bloody city! It is all full of lies and robbery; the prey departeth not;² The noise of a whip, and the noise of the rattling of the wheels, and of the prancing horses, and of the jumping chariots. ³ The horseman lifteth up both the bright sword and the glittering spear: and there is a multitude of slain, and a great number of carcasses; and there is none end of their corpses; they stumble upon their corpses:⁴ Because of the multitude of the whoredoms of the well-favored harlot, the mistress of witchcrafts, that selleth nations through her whoredoms, and families through her witchcrafts.⁵ Behold, I am against thee, saith the Lord of hosts; and I*

*will discover thy skirts upon thy face, and I will shew the nations thy
nakedness, and the kingdoms thy shame.[6] And I will cast abominable
filth upon thee, and make thee vile, and will set thee as a gazingstock.[7]
And it shall come to pass, that all they that look upon thee shall flee
from thee, and say, Nineveh is laid waste: who will bemoan her?
whence shall I seek comforters for thee?*

There could not possibly be a more wicked example, a more frightful
foe, or someone more deserving of God's wrath, so Jonah's retreat
seems sensible until we consider the *sovereign hand*, the *sincere heart*,
and the *sending call* of God. Equally moving is the incredible *spiritual
response* from this heathen nation.

Because of Jonah's obedience to proclaim the Word of the Lord, the
intended audience reacted to the message. The reaction is witnessed in
that they *heard* and *believed* God. (vs. 5). Once they heard the message
of condemnation, they immediately began the acts of repentance. We
see that little word "So" again and are reminded of the "*demonstrative
force*" of such a word. It is again speaking to a natural reflex or
something that may be or should be expected. In this instance, the
action was the sharing of the Word of God, and the reflex was to react,
and in responding, these particular people *heard* and *believed*.

While we may not form a concept or an understanding that states that
every time someone hears, they will believe… we can assume that
every time someone hears, they will react. Furthermore, we can know
that God's will in that particular moment will be activated by the
obedience to share. Nothing has changed; the lost must also *hear and
believe* if they desire salvation. But if they do not hear, they cannot
react. As the Apostle Paul asks in *Romans 10:14, "How then shall they
call on him in whom they have not believed? And how shall they*

believe in him of whom they have not heard? And how shall they hear without a preacher?"

We should also note the *intended audience responded* to the message. In *humility,* they *cried* unto God. (vs. 6-8). We see very clearly in these verses a historical account of what happened. It is not imagined, but instead it is witnessed and recorded. In this account, the audience *responded* in *humility* and *crying*! The response follows the reaction. Their response could have been to *discount* the Word of God, *dislike* the man of God, or *disagree* with God's message. But none of those things occurred. The Ninevites' response was to *humble themselves and cry out unto God*. A proper response to the guilt of sin and the recognition of the judgment of God.

This is the prescription given to Israel in *2 Chronicles 7:14 "If my people, who are called by my name, will humble themselves and seek me, then will I hear and heal their land."* Often, we apply this to America and the American way of life, but truly it is speaking of Israel; they alone have covenants and promises associated with a nation, a throne, and a land. We have a covenant associated with forgiveness, redemption, promises of Heaven, eternity, sonship, and inheritance. Israel's promises are earthly. Our promises are heavenly. Nonetheless, because of Jonah's obedience, these wicked Ninevites *hear* the message, and respond in *humility*! Today, the lost must also respond with humility if they desire Salvation. Nothing in my hand I bring, simply to thy cross I cling. Just as I am without one plea but that thy blood was shed for me. But we are all as an unclean thing, and all our righteousnesses are as filthy rags.[32] The lost must come in humility, recognizing their own need, appealing unto the saving power of the Lord Jesus Christ. Plainly stated if they do not hear they cannot respond.

The Ninevites reacted. The Ninevites responded. And the _intended audience repented_ according to the message. In repentance, they _heeded_ and _trusted_. Their trust had been in themselves, but upon hearing, they humbled themselves and repented to God by heeding the message. (vs. 9)

There is an element of faith here that is admirable at least and amazing at best. They repented and turned to God in the hope that He would relent. No promise of relenting was made unto them, and no method of redemption was described or prescribed for them. The message was, "*Yet 40 days and Nineveh will be overthrown.*" Their response was to repent, humble themselves, and hope that God would relent! (vs.9) Isn't that amazing? This godless, wicked, bloody people, satisfied and secure, hear a message of destruction from a fishy foreigner and they move to repentance and mourning in the hope that God will change his mind.

This points to the power of the word of God, preached properly. It speaks to the need for obedience, because this entire story only works if Jonah obeys God. The Ninevites can only respond with humility, contrition, hope, or faith if Jonah confronts them.

---

[32] **Isaiah 64:6** But we are all as an unclean thing, and all our righteousnesses are as filthy rags; and we all do fade as a leaf; and our iniquities, like the wind, have taken us away.

A minor problem arises in our theology in verse 10. We are told that in seeing the Ninevites' repentance, God repented. To repent, in most cases means to have "a change of mind" or "a change of heart." When we use it in the New Testament sense of the word, it speaks to a turnaround, a change of direction, and an about-face. In the salvific sense we see that we must repent from unbelief, and turn towards belief, or more appropriately turn from dependence upon self towards dependence upon God. Repentance, for mankind, always involves a change. But God is immutable. He is changeless. He cannot change. He is omniscient, all-knowing, and so how can an all-knowing God change His mind? Does this indicate that He was wrong? Or that He didn't know what would happen? Not only does this seem wrong, but the Bible also clearly states that God does not change, He does not repent, and His counsel stands forever.[33] [34] [35] [36] [37] [38] [39] [40] [41]

---

[33] **Malachi 3:6** For I am the Lord, I change not; therefore ye sons of Jacob are not consumed.

[34] **Numbers 23:19** God is not a man, that he should lie; neither the son of man, that he should repent: hath he said, and shall he not do it? or hath he spoken, and shall he not make it good?

[35] **Psalm 102:25-27** Of old hast thou laid the foundation of the earth: and the heavens are the work of thy hands.[26] They shall perish, but thou shalt endure: yea, all of them shall wax old like a garment; as a vesture shalt thou change them, and they shall be changed:[27] But thou art the same, and thy years shall have no end.

[36] **Psalm 33:11** The counsel of the Lord standeth forever, the thoughts of his heart to all generations.

[37] **Isaiah 46:10** Declaring the end from the beginning, and from ancient times the things that are not yet done, saying, My counsel shall stand, and I will do all my pleasure:

[38] **Isaiah 43:10** Ye are my witnesses, saith the Lord, and my servant whom I have chosen: that ye may know and believe me and understand that I am he: before me there was no God formed, neither shall there be after me.

[39] **Romans 11:29** For the gifts and calling of God are without repentance.

[40] **Titus 1:2** In hope of eternal life, which God, that cannot lie, promised before the world began;

[41] **Hebrews 6:17** Wherein God, willing more abundantly to shew unto the heirs of promise the immutability of his counsel, confirmed it by an oath:

So, how do we reconcile Jonah 3:10, Genesis 6:6[42], Exodus 32:14[43], Jeremiah 18:8[44], or Amos 7:3, 6[45]? In each of these verses, God repents of some intended action or of some previous action. We also see the word "relent" used in some translations. God is without sin and therefore will never need to repent from it as we do. These circumstances often arose from the intercession of a faithful man, the obedience of a called man, or the grace of God towards man. Lastly, scholars tell us that the Hebrew word used in these verses means a "strong breath" or a "sigh." The indication is that because of intercession, God sighs in relief that He will not need to carry out the intended consequence. This is precisely what happens in Jonah 3:10. Because of the obedience of Jonah in preaching the Word, the Ninevites repented from their sin, allowing God to relent from His intended actions.

What about us today? We do not preach a message of condemnation without the possibility of redemption. We do not preach a hopeless gospel. Our message is one of Hope, Promise, Forgiveness, Restoration, Redemption, Emancipation, Regeneration, and Empowerment! We needn't warn of impending doom with no chance of survival because we have a gracious heavenly Father who has given

---

[42] **Genesis 6:6** And it repented the Lord that he had made man on the earth, and it grieved him at his heart.

[43] **Exodus 32:14** And the Lord repented of the evil which he thought to do unto his people.

[44] **Jeremiah 18:8** If that nation, against whom I have pronounced, turn from their evil, I will repent of the evil that I thought to do unto them.

[45] **Amos 7:3-6** The Lord repented for this: It shall not be, saith the Lord. [4] Thus hath the Lord God shewed unto me: and behold, the Lord God called to contend by fire, and it devoured the great deep, and did eat up a part.
[5] Then said I, O Lord God, cease, I beseech thee: by whom shall Jacob arise? for he is small. [6] The Lord repented for this: This also shall not be, saith the Lord God.

His dear Son to secure our Salvation. Undoubtedly, we have a superior message; our concern is not about the message, but the messenger. The question is, are we sharing the Word of God with the intended Audience *(all the World, starting at home and reaching unto the uttermost part of the Peoples)* and providing them with the opportunity to Respond?

Consider these challenging questions.

Whereas the result of obedience to God is the accomplishment and prosperity of God's will …

… and since the Word of God will not return void but will prosper and accomplish the task unto which it is sent …

1. What should be our attitude towards witnessing?
2. Towards evangelism?
3. Towards open worship, and prayer?
4. Towards obedience to the clearly revealed desires of God.

In the words of Peter, knowing these things to be true, *"What manner of persons ought we to be?"* Why don't we make that a matter of prayer, this moment…

Heavenly Father, we desire to see the revival of thousands, the salvation of entire cities, and great movements of God. We have the message of hope and forgiveness—the only message needed to ignite the flames of revival in the darkest of places. But we are missing the messenger, the obedience, and the man who will go. Lord, here I am; send me!

"There is another salient point to keep before us as we study this book: The fish is not the hero of the story, neither is it the villain. The book is not even about a fish. The chief difficulty is in keeping a correct perspective. The fish is among the props and does not occupy the star's dressing room. Let us distinguish between the essentials and the incidentals. The incidentals are the fish, the gourd, the east wind, the boat, and Nineveh. The essentials are Jehovah and Jonah."

God and Man, J. Vernon McGee

Chapter Seven
Restored and Rewarded ... But Ungrateful

Jonah 3:10-4:4 And God saw their works, that they turned from their evil way; and God repented of the evil, that he had said that he would do unto them; and he did it not. But it displeased Jonah exceedingly, and he was very angry. And he prayed unto the Lord, and said, I pray thee, O Lord, was not this my saying, when I was yet in my country? Therefore, I fled before unto Tarshish: for I knew that thou art a gracious God, and merciful, slow to anger, and of great kindness, and repentest thee of the evil. Therefore now, O Lord, take, I beseech thee, my life from me; for it is better for me to die than to live.

In his resentment, Jonah reminds us of the ungrateful servant who, being forgiven of much, turned around and refused to forgive a little.[46] Or the self-righteous older brother who bemoaned the celebration of the returning prodigal.[47] Or the hypocritical pharisee who prayed,

---

[46] **Matthew 18:21-35**

[47] **Luke 15:25-32**

"God thank you that I am not this publican".[48] The parallel in these three examples and Jonah is ___self___. Each of these individuals (including Jonah) where more concerned with self (*comfort, care, compensation, credit, celebrity, compliment, commendation, and/or citation*) than with others – unless of course, the belittling of others meant (means) the further benefit of self. Self is often reflected in the tribe, or within tribalism, as those who are like self, similar to self, desired by self, deemed better than self, and so forth.

I realize that this concept is a hot topic in today's climate and/or culture. Unfortunately, the hot topic is frequently as tribalistic as the tribe against which it fights. Consider the following terms and definitions:

Tribalism - noun
1: tribal consciousness and loyalty
especially exaltation of the tribe above other groups
2: strong, in-group loyalty

Tribe - noun
1. a social group composed chiefly of numerous families, clans, or generations having a shared _ancestry_ and _language_.
b: a _political division_
2. a group of people having a _common character_, _occupation_, or _special interest._

Synonyms of Tribe: family- political party – house – race – people – lineage – descendants denomination – nation – region – ethnicity – dynasty – generation – folk(s) – clan – club

I am not suggesting that we should diminish the wickedness of the Ninevites and lay all of the blame at the feet of Jonah. But neither can

---

[48] **Luke 18:9-14**

we turn a blind eye to Jonah's behavior. We should never excuse bad behavior, even when the bad behavior is in response to someone else's bad behavior. I believe we should embrace the wickedness of Nineveh because it is the common denominator that unites our needs with theirs. We are just as wicked as they. Though the expression of that wickedness may be sterilized by culture, it is all filthy in God's eyes. I believe we must also embrace Jonah's poor behavior; it mirrors many of our own reactions. Once we recognize God's great forgiveness to Nineveh and Jonah, we can more accurately see the great debt Jesus paid on our accounts. Then, we may be enthused to share this magnificent gift with all who will hear, regardless of tribal affiliation.

Realizing our own wickedness, culpability, and poor behavior is the first step in repentance. Indeed, you have heard it said that "the first step in recovery is to admit there is a problem." I submit that just as *redemption, regeneration,* and *restoration* are related to *recovery, recognition* of guilt is related to *repentance.* As long as we are hyper-focused on the issues of the "other side" (*their current behavior, past behavior, personality, tendency, or simply their reported reputation*), we remain blind to our own issues, failures, and shortcomings. This is what makes us into the blind leading the blind, both of whom will end up in the pit.[49] But when we step back from the situation to gain some perspective, we'll see: there are valid issues on both sides of any conflict or disagreement.

The common issue here is that all have sinned and fallen short of the glory of God.[50] The Ninevites were a warring, wicked nation of

---

[49] **Matthew 15:14** Let them alone: they be blind leaders of the blind. And if the blind lead the blind, both shall fall into the ditch.

[50] **Romans 3:23** For all have sinned, and come short of the glory of God;

ruthless murderers. But Jonah was a cowardly, disobedient bigot who cared more about himself than he did an entire nation of people. Who is more guilty? Who is the worse criminal? Sure, the Ninevites had wiped out nations, but if Jonah refused to deliver the message of God this nation would likewise be wiped out. Jonah 4:11 states that Nineveh had one hundred and twenty thousand children, besides adults and the aged. The point is that we are all guilty; there is none righteous, no not one![51]

Notice *God's response to Nineveh's repentance*. This may be the second most important truth in this five-verse pericope of Jonah. The *response of God* is second only to the *attributes of God* in verse 2 of chapter 4. God responds immediately to the repentant attitudes and actions of the dreadful Ninevites.

God notices their actions, as the Scripture states. *He saw their repentance*. God saw their works and that they turned from their evil way. This is encouraging as it speaks to the personal aspect of a relationship with our Creator. Do you ever feel irrelevant, unnoticed, unwatched, uncared for? Do you feel like you are "just a number"? Just another droplet, among all of the other drips? Do you feel like everyone's looking for Waldo, but no one is looking for you? Well God sees everyone, from the greatest to the least. He sees their works of repentance, and He is affected. And God sees you! You are not just a number to God. He sees you. He knows you.[52] He has numbered the

---

[51] **Romans 3:10** As it is written, There is none righteous, no, not one:

[52] **Psalm 139:1-4** O lord, thou hast searched me, and known me.[2] Thou knowest my downsitting and mine uprising, thou understandest my thought afar off.[3] Thou compassest my path and my lying down, and art acquainted with all my ways.[4] For there is not a word in my tongue, but, lo, O Lord, thou knowest it altogether.

hairs on your head.[53] The old song says, *"His eyes are on the sparrow, and I know He watches me!"*

Seeing their repentance, <u>*God withholds condemnation*</u>. Seeing their works of repentance, He relents in His judgment and condemnation, which He had planned. As we have already stated, God never repents from sin, but He does relent from judgment and condemnation when He sees repentance from sin. God is not willing that anyone would perish, but that all would come to repentance,[54] and when repentance is achieved, mercy and grace overflow.[55] Knowing that God is immutable (changeless), we can rest assured that He will respond to repentance this way, even today.

Consider the wicked King Manasseh,[56] who served false gods and indulged his selfish desires. He murdered babies and prophets, and rebelled against God for more than 50 years. After defeat, and under duress he repented and humbled himself. He knew that the Lord was God, and God restored him! This is indicative of God's goodness! He

---

[53] **Matthew 10:26-31** Fear them not therefore: for there is nothing covered, that shall not be revealed; and hid, that shall not be known.[27] What I tell you in darkness, that speak ye in light: and what ye hear in the ear, that preach ye upon the housetops.[28] And fear not them which kill the body, but are not able to kill the soul: but rather fear him which is able to destroy both soul and body in hell.[29] Are not two sparrows sold for a farthing? and one of them shall not fall on the ground without your Father.[30] But the very hairs of your head are all numbered.[31] Fear ye not therefore, ye are of more value than many sparrows.

[54] **2 Peter 3:9** The Lord is not slack concerning his promise, as some men count slackness; but is longsuffering to us-ward, not willing that any should perish, but that all should come to repentance.

[55] **Numbers 14:18** The Lord is longsuffering, and of great mercy, forgiving iniquity and transgression, and by no means clearing the guilty, visiting the iniquity of the fathers upon the children unto the third and fourth generation.

[56] **2 Chronicles 33:1-19**

sees repentance and restrains condemnation! He will do this for you, even today!

Even King Nebuchadnezzar was restored.[57] He was lovingly warned by the prophet Daniel to "break off" his sins. He continued therein, and even relished his pride and accomplishments ... until he was judged and driven out by God. But when his understanding returned, Nebuchadnezzar repented and praised the Lord, and immediately he was restored. When God sees repentance, He relents from condemnation. It happens time and again throughout Scripture.

This establishes for us our next dependable concept. It is number seven. Let's review our first seven dependable concepts in the following list.

1. **God Calls every believer to serve, but not all are Compliant.**

2. **The law Convicts every person of sin, but not all are Condemned.**

3. **Every saint is Justified but not all are Just.**

4. **Every Disobedient Christian will be Disciplined.**

5. **The natural Outcome of repentance is Obedience.**

6. **Obedience Results in the accomplishment of God's Will.**

7. **When God sees Repentance, He Relents from Condemnation.**

---

[57] **Daniel 4:27** Wherefore, O king, let my counsel be acceptable unto thee, and break off thy sins by righteousness, and thine iniquities by shewing mercy to the poor; if it may be a lengthening of thy tranquility.

Moving forward the focus is solely on Jonah and his response to God's relenting, in verses one and three of Chapter Four. Actions will follow this despicable response, but for now, I want us to see Jonah's attitude. We often see similar attitudes in the church today towards evangelism, likely for similar reasons.

Jonah was displeased by Nineveh's repentance, and he was angry. Why? What displeased him? I can only believe that he was displeased with God because God did not destroy the Ninevites. That was his expectation, and it was the only thing that would have pleased him. He wanted to see their destruction. He desired to see Nineveh reap all it had sown.

The second reaction? Jonah was angry. We can only assume that he was angry that they had been given a reprieve. I suppose we could assume his anger was relative to the reversal of his prophecy, but I think it's the same selfish attitude behind both the reprieve and the reversal. Anything short of a Sodom and Gomorrah event was displeasing for Jonah. He had hoped to see total destruction and complete annihilation.

Jonah was also disconsolate. Verse three says that he preferred to die rather than face a world where God saved his enemies and reversed his prophecies. Jonah has an opportunity to claim a great victory; he can publicly praise the Lord for this amazing spiritual reversal. He could extoll the goodness of God concerning the expected outcome and the experienced outcome. But he chooses resentment as his response.

The motivation behind this resentment is tribalism. Jonah had valid reasons to hate the Ninevites. The Jews had ample reason to hate them.

More than all that Nineveh had done against Israel, there was a perception of worth. The Jews saw themselves as the *"peculiar treasure"* of God. There was the perceived righteousness of the Jew over the Ninevite. Of course, the Jews see all other nations as heathens, and as dogs. But they would have held an even higher disdain for the Assyrian empire, of which Nineveh was the capital.

I believe this perception of worth and righteousness is responsible for the handcuffing of the gospel in many situations. It is the perceived differences between groups. Those *wicked* Ninevites. Those *savage* islanders. The *impoverished* Haitians. The *Communist* Chinese. The *liberal* Europeans. The *wacky* West Coasters. The *obnoxious* New Yorkers. The *backward* Southerners. These are all cultural declarations, to create separation. While I do not have all of the answers for all of the problems, I can most definitely tell you the only valid difference between peoples is *regenerate* versus *unregenerate*. *Saved* versus *lost*. As J. Vernon McGee would say, "Some are *saints* and some are *ain'ts*." We may allow these other differentiators in our world, but God doesn't see them. He died for all who are descended from Adam. 1 John 2:2 "And he is the propitiation (atonement) for our sins: and not for ours only, but also for the sins of the whole world."

I appreciate *Jonah's representation of God's attributes* in verse two. *"Therefore, I fled."* In other words, *"This is why I fled."* This is very telling. We have contemplated Jonah's reasons for running, but now we know. He was opposed to the salvation of Nineveh. He could not fathom the Ninevites' repentance and redemption. Then, he lists all these wonderful attributes of our Savior. There is an entire sermon right here in verse two. Jonah speaks of God as gracious and merciful; he speaks of His love and compassion, that he desires to see repentance, to heal, to make whole, to resurrect the dead, and experience communion with them. And we should not see Him as a sappy lover looking for restoration, but rather a Sovereign Lord offering reconciliation![58]

Moreover, God is patient, kind, and long-suffering. He is willing to wait, He has waited, and while He waits, He continues to wait! Someone might ask, "Well, how long will He wait?" I'm not sure, but He has waited over two thousand years already. What more should we expect? If you are 20 years old, He has already waited two decades for you. If you are fifty years old, He has waited five. God is long-suffering! Why make Him wait? Repent today! Surrender to His Lordship today![59]

God is also forgiving. The blood shed upon the cross was for you, in your place, as you! It was for your forgiveness. It was for your sin debt, that you might be made the righteousness of Christ![60]

---

[58] **Ephesians 2:1-8**

[59] **Isaiah 55:6-9** Seek ye the Lord while he may be found, call ye upon him while he is near:[7] Let the wicked forsake his way, and the unrighteous man his thoughts: and let him return unto the Lord, and he will have mercy upon him; and to our God, for he will abundantly pardon.[8] For my thoughts are not your thoughts, neither are your ways my ways, saith the Lord.[9] For as the heavens are higher than the earth, so are my ways higher than your ways, and my thoughts than your thoughts.

[60] **2 Corinthians 5:17-21** Therefore if any man be in Christ, he is a new creature: old things are passed away; behold, all things are become new.[18] And all things are of God, who hath reconciled us to himself by Jesus Christ, and hath given to us the ministry of reconciliation;[19] To wit, that God was in Christ, reconciling the world unto himself, not imputing their trespasses unto them; and hath committed unto us the word of reconciliation.[20] Now then we are ambassadors for Christ, as though God did beseech you by us: we pray you in Christ's stead, be ye reconciled to God.[21] For he hath made him to be sin for us, who knew no sin; that we might be made the righteousness of God in him.

After Jonah affirms God's immutable attributes, God speaks through a simple question. Listen to _God's request for Jonah's self-audit_ in verse four. "_Doest thou well to be angry?_" Is it good for you to be angry? Is this the correct response? Are you doing the right thing? Would you deny the love of God to these people? Would you deny them the long-suffering of God? Would you deny them the forgiveness of God? Would you prefer to see them suffer and die an eternal death for their sins? Are their sins any worse than yours? Is it proper that you receive forgiveness and second chances, but they don't?

We have no problem answering that question for Jonah or perceiving his hypocrisy and hatred for feeling otherwise. But how would we respond? What is our tribal identity? Is it proper that we enjoy mercy, grace, long-suffering, and forgiveness, and one second chance after another, but others (_whom we know and see daily_) do not? Are their sins worse than ours? Does their natural birth condemn them more than ours? Do their culture, language, speech, appearance, habit life, or innate desires condemn them more than ours condemn us?

Do we do well to remain silent? One of my favorite Old Testament stories occurs in 2 Kings chapter seven. Israel is under siege by the Syrian army. They have endured a difficult season, leaving them without food and water, starving and scared. At that time, there are four lepers outside the gate awaiting death. They are outcasts (_leprosy is always a picture of sin_), unclean, rejected. The people of Israel would not have them, and the enemy would likely kill them, if they don't starve to death first. They decide it is senseless to sit there and wait for death, so they make plans to cast themselves on the mercy of the Syrians and hope for food … but willingly accept death.

When the lepers arrive at the Syrian encampment, they discover the enemy has fled during the night in fear of the Lord. They left behind all of their food, valuables, equipment, and treasures. The lepers feast on the bread and wine, hoard the silver and gold, and party and play all day long. They have the time of their lives, until their consciences come calling. In verse nine, they say to one another, "We do not well: this day is a day of good tidings, and we hold our peace: if we tarry till the morning light, some mischief will come upon us: now therefore come, that we may go and tell the king's household."[61]

This is our challenge today. We have tasted of the Lord, and He is good.[62] We have found the bread of life.[63] We have found the water that keeps us from thirsting.[64] We have found the green pastures and the still waters.[65] We have, indeed, found the Good Shepherd. And if

---

[61] **2 Kings 7:9** Then they said one to another, We do not well: this day is a day of good tidings, and we hold our peace: if we tarry till the morning light, some mischief will come upon us: now therefore come, that we may go and tell the king's household.

[62] **Psalm 34:8** O taste and see that the Lord is good: blessed is the man that trusteth in him.

[63] **John 6:35** And Jesus said unto them, I am the bread of life: he that cometh to me shall never hunger; and he that believeth on me shall never thirst.

[64] **John 4:14** But whosoever drinketh of the water that I shall give him shall never thirst; but the water that I shall give him shall be in him a well of water springing up into everlasting life.

[65] **Psalm 23** The Lord is my shepherd; I shall not want.[2] He maketh me to lie down in green pastures: he leadeth me beside the still waters.[3] He restoreth my soul: he leadeth me in the paths of righteousness for his name's sake.[4] Yea, though I walk through the valley of the shadow of death, I will fear no evil: for thou art with me; thy rod and thy staff they comfort me.[5] Thou preparest a table before me in the presence of mine enemies: thou anointest my head with oil; my cup runneth over.[6] Surely goodness and mercy shall follow me all the days of my life: and I will dwell in the house of the Lord forever.

we are not actively telling everyone we meet, we must say, just as these four lepers determined themselves, we do not do well today!

Have you experienced regeneration? Have you been born again? Would you prevent anyone else from enjoying the same benefit you have freely received? Who have you told? Who have you prayed for? Who have you witnessed this?

Father, we come now with a burning conscience. We know that we have not done well. Lord, we ask first for forgiveness for our sin of lethargy. Next, Lord, we seek opportunity to speak, share, and shout the good news. Father, would you give us the boldness to fulfill your will? Lord, would you help us to see others as You see them? Help us to remember the ground is level at the foot of the cross! Help us defeat tribalism in our own life. Amen

"One minute he's preaching God's Word, the next minute he's disobeying it and leaving his post of duty. While inside the great fish, he prayed to be delivered, but now he asks the Lord to kill him. He called the city to repentance, but he wouldn't repent himself... The Ninevites, the vine, the worm, and the wind have all obeyed God, but Jonah refuses to obey, and he has the most to gain."
Warren Wiersbe

Chapter Eight
Invited to Rejoice ... But Sulking

Jonah 4:4-11 Then said the Lord, Doest thou well to be angry? So, Jonah went out of the city, and sat on the east side of the city, and there made him a booth, and sat under it in the shadow, till he might see what would become of the city. And the Lord God prepared a gourd, and made it to come up over Jonah, that it might be a shadow over his head, to deliver him from his grief. So, Jonah was exceeding glad of the gourd. But God prepared a worm when the morning rose the next day, and it smote the gourd that it withered. And it came to pass, when the sun did arise, that God prepared a vehement east wind; and the sun beat upon the head of Jonah, that he fainted, and wished in himself to die, and said, It is better for me to die than to live. And God said to Jonah, Doest thou well to be angry for the gourd? And he said, I do well to be angry, even unto death. Then said the Lord, Thou hast had pity on the gourd, for the which thou hast not labored, neither madest it grow; which came up in a night, and perished in a night: And should not I spare Nineveh, that great city, wherein are more than six score thousand persons that cannot discern between their right hand and their left hand; and also much cattle?

We will complete our study of the man Jonah with this final installment of eight verses and then one more chapter on the *restrictions of time*. Before we read our passage and consider God's restorative desires. Take a moment to review some of these dependable concepts that we have established. I believe they are current and applicable to the modern believer.

1. **God calls every believer to serve, but not all are compliant.**

2. **The law convicts every person, but not all are condemned.**

3. **Every saint is justified but not all are just.**

4. **Every disobedient Christian will be disciplined.**

5. **The natural outcome of repentance is obedience.**

6. **Obedience results in the accomplishment of God's will.**

7. **When God sees repentance, He relents from condemnation.**

When we see and agree with these concepts, we are challenged in several ways...

We should be compliant/obedient in our Christian walk.
We should expect discipline/chastisement when we are not.
The proper response to discipline is repentance, not resistance.
Repentance from disobedience is simply obedience.
God's will begins with Obedience.
Obedience accomplishes and prospers God's will.
When we repent, God forgives. (We are never beyond repentance)

The next dependable concept we will learn from Jonah is in the title of the chapter…

8.   The chief Desire of God for man is Restoration.

In this section, we see God's very personal, even conversant involvement with Jonah. We also have three separate questions directed from God unto Jonah. This paragraph opens with a question and closes with a question. Interestingly, someone has pointed out that the entire book of Jonah begins with a call and closes with a question.

Can I tell you that this is not unlike your Christian life? If you are born-again, it is because you felt the call of God upon your life; your attention was called to the knock on the door. Revelation 3:20 says, "Behold, I stand at the door, and knock; if any man hear my voice I will come in unto him, and sup with him, and he with me." If you are born-again, you allowed Him to come in. If we were speaking of your life right now, would you readily say, "I have let Him in"?

This passage shows that Jonah's attitude worsens, while God's desires remain unchanged. Jonah looks like some of us in verse five; he is pouting, he is displeased with all that has taken place, and at some level, he still hopes for destruction, as he waits and watches to see what becomes of Nineveh. Theologians will tell you that the 40 days had not yet elapsed at this time, and Jonah still hoped that condemnation would fall. In his pouting, we can see reflections of ourselves when he seeks isolation out of the city, away from the Ninevites, putting distance between himself and whatever damage may come. If we consider that Nineveh was on the banks of the Tigris, then likely the elevation increased, the further east Jonah travels. So, he ascends away from those wicked Ninevites. This is a difficult position for the concerned Christian who is also a compassionate evangelist. We are to practice godly separation without becoming isolated. We are to be in the World, but not of the World.[66] Salt and light can do no good if they are locked away from darkness and need.

We must also be wise in our approach. We do not want to use the least of us (*our children, or those who are still babes in Christ – young in the faith*) as cannon fodder (*soldiers regarded merely as material to be expended in war*) to witness to others. We must develop ourselves and others as soldiers of the cross through discipline and discipleship.[67] Who else can stand against the wiles of Satan,[68] in love and compassion towards the lost?[69]

---

[66] **John 15:19-20** If ye were of the world, the world would love his own: but because ye are not of the world, but I have chosen you out of the world, therefore the world hateth you.[20] Remember the word that I said unto you, The servant is not greater than his lord. If they have persecuted me, they will also persecute you; if they have kept my saying, they will keep yours also.

[67] **2 Timothy 2:3-6** Thou therefore endure hardness, as a good soldier of Jesus Christ.[4] No man that warreth entangleth himself with the affairs of this life; that he may please him who hath chosen him to be a soldier. [5] And if a man also strive for masteries, yet is he not crowned, except he strive lawfully.[6] The husbandman that laboureth must be first partaker of the fruits.

[68] **Ephesians 6:11-13** Put on the whole armor of God, that ye may be able to stand against the wiles of the devil.[12] For we wrestle not against flesh and blood, but against principalities, against powers, against the rulers of the darkness of this world, against spiritual wickedness in high places.[13] Wherefore take unto you the whole armor of God, that ye may be able to withstand in the evil day, and having done all, to stand.

[69] **Ephesians 4:32** And be ye kind one to another, tenderhearted, forgiving one another, even as God for Christ's sake hath forgiven you.

Do we isolate ourselves? Are we guilty of avoiding the need? Do we place distance between ourselves and the possible damage of condemnation?

When Jonah finally stopped, he displayed his _independence_. He made himself a booth and sat under the shadow of it. It was a booth for one – single occupancy. Just enough room for one man and his ego. Jonah didn't need anyone to do it for him, or with him; he could do it himself. He would enjoy this position of spite and bitterness all by his little lonesome.

We know this man today. He is independent. He doesn't need the church, friends, family; he doesn't need anyone. In fact, he is so independent he may not even need God.

Jonah also displays indignation. This is the contempt he holds for the Ninevites – his desire to see their ruin, condemnation, and destruction. He isn't introspective about his own disobedience, delinquency, discipline, repentance, or restoration. He simply sees himself as chosen of God, and others as less deserving of God's grace and mercy, patience, kindness, and deliverance. He sits back to watch and wait for the deserved destruction of the wicked with the full confidence of his own deliverance as his cushion.

This is Jonah's devolving attitude. And it is the same attitude of many who occupy cushioned seats in church houses across our nation today. They are isolated from the problem, independent of the body that works to resolve the need, and indignant towards the lost and the calamity that awaits them.

Next, let's consider the prepared things (vs. 6-8) God prepared the Great Wind, and the Great Fish. I believe the great wind was for exposure, and the great fish was for export. The former revealed where Jonah was, while the latter removed Jonah to where he was supposed to be. In these next few verses, three more prepared things appear.

First is the Gourd, which was for comfort. I am confident that the shade of this living thing was cool and comfortable. I would imagine that Jonah even felt blessed by God that it had grown, though he never said so. God winked at him with this plant that grew up from nothing in the middle of nowhere, in no time at all. Jonah was glad, but not specifically towards God.

There is no thanksgiving or sigh of relief for the care of God. Jonah only shows temporary gladness for carnal comfort. Paul, speaking in Romans 2:4 concerning the commonality of guilt across the range of humanity, says that God's goodness is meant to lead us to repentance. "Or do you presume on the riches of his kindness and forbearance and patience, not knowing that God's kindness is meant to lead you to repentance?" What comfort has God placed in your life to help you repent from a faulty attitude or failing actions?

Then there is the Worm, which was for contradiction. The worm destroyed the comfort of the gourd, creating an atmosphere of contradiction to lead to conviction. We have heard folks say "The Lord gives, and the Lord takes away."[70] When we consider that verse's context in the Book of Job, we must see it through the lens of God's

---

[70] **Job 1:21** And said, Naked came I out of my mother's womb, and naked shall I return thither: the Lord gave, and the Lord hath taken away; blessed be the name of the Lord.

sovereignty. We get another view of this same filter in James 1, where we are warned of the developing desires of God through trials and difficulties. But in the same chapter, we are also warned of the destructive intentions of the enemy through temptations. In James 1:17, we read "Every good and perfect gift is from above… coming down from the Father." The concept is that in the sovereignty of God, sometimes he gives for blessing and sometimes takes for teaching or instruction or to bring about confrontation.

We are prone to bitterness over losing that comfort or blessing, which is exactly how Jonah responds. He was "angry, even unto death" over the loss of the gourd. Imagine if Jonah would have thanked God for the provision of comfort, and sought God over the contradiction. Imagine if Jonah would have felt God's heart in this event!

What has God been showing you through contradiction? Where has He revealed that you are compromised? What is more important to you than the salvation of the lost?

The Lord also sent the vehement East wind, which was for conviction. The hot wind withered away comfort and pushed Jonah to a place of response. The wind impacted him physically and emotionally. He was fatigued and faint and felt as if he would die. He believed death would be better than this form of living.

In today's church environment, folks will leave if the teaching and preaching are too convicting. They will classify it as too intense, heavy, dark, or serious. And they will seek a place that assures them of their eventual glory, immediate goodness, and issues unto them the generous grace of God, for today, lacking any responsibility. We should not run from conviction. Instead, we should *realize* it, *respond* to it, and *repent* of it. It is the goodness of God that brings repentance. True conviction brings sorrow, and Godly sorrow worketh repentance.[71] Have you run from conviction? Resisted? Turned a blind eye towards it?

Finally, God in love asks penetrating questions. (vs. 4, 9-11) Three times in these verses, the Lord poses a question to Jonah. Each was an opportunity to repent and embrace the work God was performing among the Ninevites. Each was an attempt by God to bring restoration full circle to Jonah. His first question is, "Consider yourself." Is this the correct response? Would you deny God's love, long-suffering and forgiveness to these people? Would you see them suffer and die for their sins? Are their sins any worse than yours? Is it proper that you receive forgiveness and second chances, but they don't? God is providing for introspection – an inward look at self, a remembering of the past, and the personal salvation that God has provided.

The second question: "Consider your surroundings." (vs. 9) God effectively says, "Jonah, look at the blessings in your life, everything I provided for you. And you are yet hardhearted towards others who have not had such blessings. You did not toil fruitlessly; I rewarded your toil, and you have been blessed." He is providing for reflection. Think of all of God's goodness in your life. Should other people expire without the same goodness?

Finally, God asks, "Consider the souls." (vs. 10-11) This is really the coup de grace or final blow. This should be the question,

---

[71] **2 Corinthians 7:10** For godly sorrow worketh repentance to salvation not to be repented of: but the sorrow of the world worketh death.

consideration, and motivation for everything we believe, think, say, and do. What about other people? What about their eternal souls? It is bad enough to live, struggle, suffer, and die. Should they suffer eternally? Should we not be compassionate enough *to pray*, *to pay*, to *participate*, to *push*, to *pursue* evangelism, to seek and fulfill the Great Commission, and the *"populating"* of Heaven with all who will believe?

You may say, "Well, aren't we doing this?"

It depends on what you base your decisions upon. Are you motivated by self, surroundings, or lost souls? Are you more focused on comfort, or compliance? Do you consider yourself better than others by any standard other than the *Grace of God*? Is there a group you believe to be beyond the reach of the gospel?

One soul is of more value than the whole world; surely then one soul is of more value than many gourds: we should have more concern for our own and others' precious souls, than for the riches and enjoyments of this world.
Matthew Henry

Now that you have the truth, it's time for a response. Your response may be, based upon the blessings of God, to repent and believe the Gospel, confess Christ as your Lord and Savior, and seek to be obedient to Him. Or your response may be to remember the grace of God that has forgiven and regenerated you, and it's time to begin your quest for the souls of man. There are many possible responses, I suppose. But I am certain that one is specifically due from you.

Heavenly Father, I pray for conviction, not comfort. I pray for contradiction and not complacency. God give me a heart for the souls and a motivation to share the truth with anyone who will hear! Amen

"If someone had told me when I was 20 years old that life was very short and that it would pass just like 'that,' I wouldn't have believed it. And if I don't tell you that, you don't believe it either. The fact that time is short calls for something now. The things we ought to do, the classes we ought to take, the books we ought to read—do it now!
... Time is too short for indecision."
Billy Graham

Chapter Nine
Called and Expected Today

We have established a healthy list of principles.

1. **God calls every believer to serve, but not all are compliant.**

2. **The law convicts every person, but not all are condemned.**

3. **Every saint is justified but not all are just.**

4. **Every disobedient Christian will be disciplined.**

5. **The natural outcome of repentance is obedience.**

6. **Obedience results in the accomplishment of God's will.**

7. **When God sees repentance, He relents from condemnation.**

8. **The chief Desire of God for man is Restoration.**

The ninth and final dependable principle is…

9. **The Restriction of Time. Today is the day for Repentance.**

The message that Jonah was instructed to deliver, and indeed delivered to the Ninevites, was a simplistic warning of impending judgment. As we have stated, the entire message consists of just eight words, which is the simplest understanding. *"Yet forty days, and Nineveh shall be overthrown."* No offer of repentance, no opportunity for forgiveness, no other alternative. Just an announcement, with a shelf life of 40 days. But of course, the Ninevites did repent, in sackcloth and ashes, in hopes of clemency. God recognized their repentance and granted them the forgiveness they had hoped for. Lesson learned… Right?

Not so quick. Why 40 days? What is the significance of that number? What if they had waited 41 days? Would that have made a difference? What truth can we learn from this? And what application might we make today?

The number 40 turns out to be a common number in the scriptures. It recurs from Genesis to the Book of Acts. In fact, one source states that it appears 159 times in the Bible across both Testaments.

It rained 40 days and 40 nights in the flood. Moses was 40 when he fled Egypt. He tended the flock for 40 years before his call. He led the nation of Israel for 40 years through the wilderness. He was on the mountain with the Lord for 40 days and 40 nights. He dispatched the spies into Canaan for 40 days. This all occurs in the Pentateuch alone.

Saul, David, and Solomon reigned as Kings of Israel for 40 years each. Goliath taunted the armies of Israel for 40 days before David slew him. The prophet Ezekiel once lay on his right side for 40 days to bear the sins of Judea. This all occurs in the Old Testament alone.

Christ fasted for 40 days in the wilderness to begin His ministry. He also appeared for 40 days after His resurrection. Forty years after the crucifixion, the temple was destroyed. Some have calculated 40 generations from Adam to the first advent of Christ, aka the fullness of time. The Scriptures are replete with the usage of the number 40. In most cases, it is agreed that 40 is the number of probation, testing, and trials. If this is true, it makes sense that Nineveh was given a 40-day window of judgment. Even though there was no prescribed repentance, there was undoubtedly an opportunity for it, and obviously, repentance was undertaken, and the Lord could discern the Ninevites' sincerity.

This explains why the number was 40, but it doesn't explain why there was a delay. If Nineveh was so wicked, and their wickedness had come up before the Lord, and He had moved to send Jonah to them with the judgment … why wait 40 days? Why not two days, or 10, or 20? Two answers deserve consideration. The first is that God is a God of order; He does things the way He chooses. One of the results of the sin curse is chaos and confusion. These things are not of God; they result from the sin curse upon this world. The second is that God is a long-suffering God. He is not willing for anyone to perish but for all to repent—even the wicked Ninevites.

With a clear grasp of the meaning and reason for the 40 days, let's consider it a challenge. Whether you are more like Jonah or Nineveh, have you responded to the call of God in your life with a sense of urgency, understanding that while God is a God of Grace, He is also a God of order, dependability, and deadlines? The grace of God has a shelf life. His long-suffering has a limit. Waiting for a more convenient time to respond may just be a death sentence for you. It may be a complete disqualifier for you. The time to respond is now.

Even the Lord Jesus said, "I must work the works of him that sent me, while it is day: the night cometh, when no man can work."[72] He was God in the flesh, but He was urgent in accomplishing His Father's will. Paul tells us that we should walk wisely and not as fools and that we must redeem the time because the days are evil![73] And James, the Lord's brother, tells us that we must not depend upon tomorrow because our life is a vapor that is here for a while and then vanishes away.[74] And lastly, Isaiah says that we must seek the Lord while He may be found and call upon Him while He is near.[75]

What is keeping you from responding favorably and obediently unto the Lord today? Is it your pride? Your anger? Your ego? Your prejudice?

In Exodus, the Lord covered Egypt with frogs. When Pharaoh realized he could not make the frogs disappear, he sought Moses' intercession with the Lord. Moses asked Pharaoh when he would like for the frogs

[72] **John 9:4**

[73] **Ephesians 5:15-21**

[74] **James 4:14**

[75] **Isaiah 55:6-9** Seek ye the Lord while he may be found, call ye upon him while he is near: 7 Let the wicked forsake his way, and the unrighteous man his thoughts: and let him return unto the Lord, and he will have mercy upon him; and to our God, for he will abundantly pardon. 8 For my thoughts are not your thoughts, neither are your ways my ways, saith the Lord. 9 For as the heavens are higher than the earth, so are my ways higher than your ways, and my thoughts than your thoughts.

to depart, and his choice was tomorrow…[76] He is enduring a plague from God but is willing to wait until tomorrow to have it removed. Is that you? Are you enduring something uncomfortable, unclean, unnatural, or unnecessary, but because of a lack of urgency, you are willing to tolerate it just a little longer?

Whether your need is one of redemption or restoration, would you pray today… right this minute?

Heavenly Father, give me, I pray thee, a sense of urgency for your call, your commands, and your commission. Lord, give me a clear vision to see my needs and the needs of those around me and a burning desire to accomplish all that I can today and each day moving forward.

---

[76] **Exodus 8:8-10** Then Pharaoh called for Moses and Aaron, and said, Intreat the Lord, that he may take away the frogs from me, and from my people; and I will let the people go, that they may do sacrifice unto the Lord. 9 And Moses said unto Pharaoh, Glory over me: when shall I intreat for thee, and for thy servants, and for thy people, to destroy the frogs from thee and thy houses, that they may remain in the river only?10 And he said, Tomorrow. And he said, Be it according to thy word: that thou mayest know that there is none like unto the Lord our God.

Conclusion

"Lord, make me less like Jonah and more like Jesus. Save me from being the kind of person who cares more about my comfort, reputation, and success than I do about the people You are calling me to serve. Help me keep all of my dreams on Your altar and be ready to respond with faith and obedience to Your call."
Colin S. Smith

We can glean several lessons from the consumption of the Jonah narrative. We list the gleanings as eight dependable concepts. Or we mention them as seven challenges to our conduct. We may consider the cultural implications, the nastiness of the Assyrians, and the religious arrogance of the Jews. We might consider the man Jonah. Why did he choose to run from his calling? We ponder what he may have witnessed as a child that would make him so prejudiced against the Ninevites. We wonder why he chose the ship, what was in his mind as he slept, or how he envisioned the "overboard experience" would be. We consider the sailors and the difficult position they found themselves in. We imagine their life after this event. Did they continue to worship the one true God? Or did they just add Him to their extensive list of gods? These are likely the everyday thoughts.

But shouldn't we be interested in learning from Jonah? Shouldn't we seek to be like Jesus? Shouldn't we determine to learn from the example of this pitiful prophet?

There is a very clear dichotomy between Jonah and Jesus. The former protects himself, while the latter practices humility and obedience. The Apostle Paul speaks to us in his letter to the Philippians, an epistle written to believers. His encouragement in chapter two is that we model ourselves after Christ Jesus.

Philippians 2:5-8 *Let this mind be in you, which was also in Christ Jesus:* [6] *Who, being in the form of God, thought it not robbery to be equal with God:* [7] *But made himself of no reputation, and took upon him the form of a servant, and was made in the likeness of men:* [8] *And being found in fashion as a man,* <u>*he humbled himself, and became*</u> <u>*obedient*</u> *unto death, even the death of the cross.*

The chief encouragement is to seek the same mind, thought process, desires, attitude, or intentions that the Lord Jesus Christ possessed. Then there is the description of the process whereby He, Jesus, modeled this for us. Notice that it begins with His perception of self and position. Jesus is the eternal Son, the second person of the Trinity, and He is God. As John teaches,[77] He was in the beginning with God, and He was God, and by Him all things were created. In John 1:14[78], we are told that He became flesh and dwelt among us. This is Jesus, the God-man, the one mediator between God and man.[79] But we see that even though He is God, He did not cling to that *position*, or that identity if you will, but rather came to deliver us, sacrificing Himself and His *position*.

---

[77] **John 1:1-5** In the beginning was the Word, and the Word was with God, and the Word was God. [2] The same was in the beginning with God. [3] All things were made by him; and without him was not anything made that was made. [4] In him was life; and the life was the light of men. [5] And the light shineth in darkness; and the darkness comprehended it not.

[78] **John 1:14** And the Word was made flesh, and dwelt among us, (and we beheld his glory, the glory as of the only begotten of the Father,) full of grace and truth.

[79] **1 Timothy 2:5** For there is one God, and one mediator between God and men, the man Christ Jesus;

To accomplish this, He humbled Himself and became obedient. This is exactly what Jonah had to do: He had to humble himself and become obedient to God's call to "Go to Nineveh and cry against it." But even though he did it, his attitude remained focused on himself, his needs, and his desires.

The message is that all believers are called to serve, but not everyone serves because some are disobedient. A Christian can be convicted of sin without being condemned, and every Christian is justified, but not all are living a just life. These disobedient children of God will be disciplined; this should bring about repentance, and repentance from disobedience is obedience. When we are obedient to the call of God, the will of God is accomplished. This shows that when God sees repentance, He relents from the discipline or condemnation.

For the unregenerate man who is dead in trespasses and sin [80] repentance brings the restoration of life.

For the regenerate man who has broken his communication with God, repentance brings a restoration of fellowship.

In every case, God's chief desire for mankind is restoration.

Will you be restored?

---

[80] **Ephesians 2:1** And you hath he quickened, who were dead in trespasses and sins;

About the Author

Cory Sexton pastors Hoschton Baptist Church in Hoschton, Georgia, where he's served in leadership since 2012. He oversaw a decade of significant growth for the church, including the purchase of a 30-acre property and multiple building projects.

Cory attributes the success and impetus behind Your Church Needs You to the selfless, sacrificial commitment of the many lay members who call Hoschton their home church. In 2023 he created a Scriptural and ethical framework for church engagement called *Heroic Church Membership* - now *Your Church Needs You*, which he turned into a sermon series. An eponymous book version soon followed.

Cory regularly speaks to like-minded audiences, challenging them to rise up and answer the needs of their local churches. He's been married to his wife, Karla, for 34 years, and together they have two children — Kayla, 31, and Carter, 26. In his spare time, Cory enjoys hunting, football and spending time with his family.

More from Cory Sexton:
Your Church Needs You calls on believers everywhere to return to the rewarding power and impact of dedicated Christian service.

Learn more at PublishWithEmissary.com/Cory-Sexton

www.ingramcontent.com/pod-product-compliance
Lightning Source LLC
Chambersburg PA
CBHW070437130626
46553CB00006B/2229